IMPERFECT
HEART

A Journal, a Book Club, and a Global Pandemic

ALSO BY TONI FUHRMAN

Only Yesterday

A Windless Place

The Second Mrs. Price

One Who Loves

IMPERFECT HEART

A Journal, a Book Club, and a Global Pandemic

TONI FUHRMAN

A WINDLESS PLACE

ISBN 979-8-9904662-0-3

First paperback edition 2024

Editor Barbara Lanctot
Cover designer Judith San Nicolas
Interior designer Lorie DeWorken
Author photo Jennifer Skelly & Auston James

Author website: https://tonifuhrman.com

Printed in the United States of America

A Windless Place Publishing
P. O. Box 291015
Los Angeles, CA, USA 90029

A WINDLESS PLACE

For Barbara Lanctot, friend and editor.

"Like failure, chaos contains information that can lead to knowledge—even wisdom."

Toni Morrison

Preface

Imperfect Heart: A Journal, a Book Club, and a Global Pandemic was written between April 2020 and December 2021. Every entry is dated; every entry was written in chronological order, including the fictional story I refer to as "the book club."

My intention was to chronicle my personal reflections in the moment, and events as they happened. I did not alter the entries in any way to reflect subsequent events more accurately—even though subsequent events may have substantiated my entries.

This is a personal account of my experience—that of sheltering in place during a time of historical significance: a pandemic that would, over the course of less than two years, take the lives of millions globally. As I began writing, however, I became equally immersed in chronicling the political and social upheaval within our country that accompanied the pandemic and grew in tandem with it.

While I was always alert to outside events, there is a lot of "me" in the book as well. This comes under the journal heading and is personal and discursive, a style that mirrored my mood in the moment of writing and reflecting. Looking back, I see a lurch back to my Catholic beginnings—a result, no doubt, of the very real fear of not surviving the pandemic.

I wrote about the book club because it helped me through those solitary months. Like Indi, my LBD (little brown dog) and constant companion, the book club was with me throughout. I looked forward to visiting, month after month, that close little group of four, trying to better understand what was happening in the world by looking into their minds and hearts, and reading and analyzing the books they were reading and analyzing.

I have written what is called a "hybrid" work. The term was not in my literary vocabulary as I wrote this, but it seems to fit. What I knew, as I began this work, was that I wanted to combine chronicle, personal reflection, memoir, and fiction. What became increasingly clear to me, as I wrote from day to day, was how closely the political chaos unleashed in our country corresponded to and reflected *"the fatal breath"* * of the pandemic.

Toni Fuhrman
January 2024

---

* a reference to *A Journal of the Plague Year* (1722) by Daniel Defoe, one of the books discussed by the book club.

IMPERFECT
HEART

A Journal, a Book Club, and a Global Pandemic

Prologue

I call upon my imperfect heart to tell the story.

We are living in the unknown center of a viral pandemic. I am, it seems, among the most vulnerable, counted among the older population, living on "borrowed time," so to speak, perhaps approaching my expiration date.

There's something else. I have what is called a "preexisting condition."

It is my imperfect heart.

Despite being a potential host for this invisible predator, I may survive. While I am surviving, I will continue to see, hear, smell, taste, touch—although the latter, among my fellow human beings, is not conducive to continuing health.

Most of all, I will continue to feel.

Perhaps because of my age, or my isolation, I am leaning toward the philosophical. How fitting that it is my heart that may crack or break! I have been challenging it and risking it most of my life. It may, in this unthinkable crisis, take its toll. There seems to be no way to prepare for this crisis except to meet it head-on. I am physically isolated, mentally unsettled, on an emotional seesaw. But I am ready to take it on, this life of mine, these feelings of mine, this time of mine. I will call upon my imperfect heart to tell the story.

April 1, 2020

To begin.

An estimated 675,000 Americans died of influenza during the 1918 pandemic. The pandemic infected 500 million people—about a quarter of the world's population at the time. The death toll is estimated to have been anywhere from 20 million to 50 million, and possibly as high as 100 million. It was one of the deadliest pandemics in human history.

Until now.

Our lives will never again be the same.

This thought has been with me, day after day, for weeks. I have to say it "out loud," so that I can rid myself of its incessant *thrump* in my head.

There appears to be, for me at least, a different sense of time, and a sort of mental muddle that has to do with both personal anxiety and the growing global catastrophe. Much of this has to do with isolation. The days meld into one another. I have to look at my iPhone to remind myself of the hour of the day, the day of the week. Everything has slowed down, in a way—and yet time seems to have speeded up; the hours of the day disappear as I move from one mental or physical activity to another—from writing, answering email, checking up on family and friends, to news gathering, tackling bills, day-to-day housekeeping, preparing meals—to a blessed hour or so of reading in the late evening, or meditating on the abrupt and drastic turn our lives have taken.

I think in terms of wartime rationing when I contemplate my small store of goods. Who knows if or when more of any one item will be available? Paper goods are scarce.

Antiseptic products have disappeared from store shelves and online retail outlets. In a new and starkly palpable way, we are dependent on an army of men and women to keep our hospitals and clinics running, our medications and other medical help available, our neighborhoods safe, our lines of communication open, our utilities and technology functioning; to plant and harvest our foods, manufacture and distribute the goods we need, stock and restock our stores, check out our groceries, deliver our mail and packages, keep the gas stations open. We can no longer take for granted that these services will be available when we wake up tomorrow morning. The day-to-day services we depend on entail an inherent and unprecedented level of risk for those who provide these services.

Of course, at some point, perhaps as early as 2021, our lives will achieve a new normalcy. We will have lost untold numbers of lives. We will all know personally those infected by, hopefully recovered from, the virus. Our older population will be diminished. We will be physically interacting in strange, unfamiliar ways. We will gather in large crowds with apprehension. The friendly handshake, high-five, hug, kiss on the cheek, will have largely disappeared. We will attend and/or host social gatherings with care. We will interact with our work associates with even more care. Sexual contact will be affected by this inherent constraint, perhaps taking a personal toll. We will shop for our basic needs under the shadow of the pandemic. We will hoard. We will be prepared, like global catastrophe preppers, for the next crisis in our lives. For some of us, that includes firearms. We will understand our connection with each other with heightened insight and hindsight. But we will also be more selfish, more centered on our family and friends, more cognizant of our need for those people in our lives who give a damn about whether we live or die.

We will no longer be as we were.

I think about, wonder about, what we will have lost. The loss of lives is a given, so tragically amplified by a hopelessly ineffectual national leader. From 2016 through 2019, we watched the unfolding of the "Trump Reality Show" (my term) as it played out in the national theater and affected everyone in the national audience. Back then, we could rant endlessly about the man who would be President of the United States and somehow got there, but we had a hope-at-the-end-of-the-road mentality. We would get rid of him in 2020. We would vote him out of our lives.

We'll never get rid of him now. He may be defeated seven months from now, but we will bear the stigma of his legacy with lives altered and lives lost. Donald Trump is the living embodiment of the pandemic, a man who has infected each of us with the virus of his greed, ignorance, and malevolence as surely as Covid-19 is infecting us at this very moment.

More tragic than the infection, though, is the loss of life—the devastating result of our president's indifference to and lack of empathy for any human being not in that room of wall-to-wall mirrors and a television set that comprises most of the space inside his head. Referring to the potential loss of American lives in a recent press briefing, Trump surmised that a death toll of 100,000 "is a very low number," adding, "if we can hold that down to 100,000," we will have done "a very good job."

The 1918 pandemic began in early 1918 and lasted, in several waves, until 1920. Cycling through multiple waves and iterations, our current pandemic may very well last as long. We'll find a vaccine. We'll build our immunities. We'll carry on. Unfortunately, there is no Trump vaccine. We must inoculate ourselves.

April 4, 2020

For the most part, I watch and listen to MSNBC. I read *The Los Angeles Times* and *The New York Times*. I also watch PBS and listen to NPR—and I tune into ABC, CBS, NBC, and CNN. I never watch Fox, although I may pick up a story or two in my daily news rounds.

Are there any Fox watchers tuning in to MSNBC? I doubt it. They're getting their version of the news; I'm getting mine. The news reporters and analysts reinforce our existing beliefs and opinions. My convictions remain the same.

Are we preaching to the choir?

"Their" convictions remain the same. Nothing changes. Trump has 75 million unquestioning minions. The rest of us push on, reassuring each other, sharing our anger, our anxiety, our hope.

MSNBC may be preaching to the choir, but I'm grateful for it, on a daily, hourly basis.

April 8, 2020

On April 1, I began keeping two notes on my Calendar: "What am I doing today?" in red (that's my To Do color) and "What did I do today?" in purple (that's my Personal color). It's mostly trivial details, but also some notes that may be useful going forward. Everything is changing so quickly that it's hard to keep track of day-to-day news and events. I woke up this morning to the news that Bernie Sanders has dropped out of the presidential race.

I would like to say I get up, brush my teeth, take care of Indi (my dog), make a cup of coffee, and sit down to write—but that's not the case these days. Outside events are too important to ignore until the end of the day, as I did in my previous life as a writer.

Also, I'm eventually going to go broke; my finances are a persistent buzz in my head. That buzz never turns off completely. It's just another source of anxiety. What I know: I'll make it with a razor-thin margin through the next few months, perhaps beyond. After that, the cupboard is bare, the bills—many of which I've managed to postpone with my daily calls—will go unpaid or partially paid.

Every detail of every aspect of my life, and that of my family and friends, has become important in an outsize way—perhaps because every day is so perilous. This is what it feels like to be living in a state of war, and this pandemic is World War III. Sickness and death are random, unpredictable. All we can do is protect our loved ones and ourselves, and watch, and wait.

April 10, 2020

I sit at my desk. It's past 9:00 a.m. I tune in MSNBC on my iPhone. I listen to Governor Andrew Cuomo as his daily report is televised. I call him "President" Cuomo because his reports give me the information I'm hungry for. He says the New York curve is flattening. He's cautiously optimistic. He says we need the Federal Production Act to get on top of the testing. Our president will not invoke the FPA. Cuomo is careful not to express his frustration with the federal government. He has to be careful. The sitting president must be appeased because he holds the power. I hear that coronavirus deaths have passed 100,000 globally, and that, here at home, states are battling for protective gear "in a market driven by chaos and fear."

⌣⁀

It's Good Friday. I'm thinking about my religious beliefs, my religious lack of belief, my lack of religious practice. I have never abandoned my religion, even though I haven't been to a religious service for years, even though the last time I was in a Catholic church was, as I recall, a visit to a local historical mission. I've asked in my health directive for the last rites, if possible, and a Catholic burial.

I am a Roman Catholic born and bred. From grades one through eight, I was taught by Notre Dame nuns in the school across the street from my home. I went to a Jesuit university, where I minored in religion, philosophy, and history. I have a Catholic conscience, a Catholic sensibility. I find solace in the possibility of a God, but my belief is more

Eastern. I believe that God resides within each of us, that "God" and "soul" are synonymous, that my body is holy because it houses the God within me.

I want to find some way to observe Good Friday, Holy Saturday, and Easter Sunday as a Catholic. I feel a need for reaching back, reaching in, to that place within me that believes, to that part of my psyche that needs to believe.

It's just ahead of 11:00 a.m. The White House briefing is about to begin. I turn off my iPhone as the president comes to the podium. I don't want to look at him. I don't want to hear his voice. My anger is overwhelming. I am not a Catholic at this moment. I don't forgive him. I can't forgive him. I have no sympathy for one who has no empathy, no compassion, no conscience, no sense of history, no perspective beyond himself and his political agenda. The man who, for me, is the embodiment of the pandemic is about to spew his hatred and ignorance on his sycophants and those of us who cannot yet rid ourselves of his malevolent presence. I'll find out what I need to know later, from the news, from analysts I trust, from Governor Cuomo.

It's noon. I'm observing Good Friday by reserving the hours of 12:00 to 3:00 p.m. for silence, meditation, and writing.

⌣

I just looked up my childhood home. It was built in 1910, measures 2,536 square feet, and sits on a 0.36-acre lot that extends from the front street to the street behind the house. When the house was built, it was a single-unit house surrounded, I was told, by a wrought-iron fence. The fence was probably a contribution to the WWI war effort. I only knew the house when it had been converted into a double unit. On both sides, the first-floor windows facing the street are long and narrow. I always liked those windows.

My great-uncle Doc bought this property, then rented it to my parents, then sold it to them. Uncle Doc lived with my grandparents up the street from our house. He and my grandmother grew up in the house one door further up the street. My grandma, who had a wicked sense of humor, used to say that she lived at home doing housework for more than twenty years; then got married, moved next door, and did the same thing for the rest of her life.

After my grandparents married, Uncle Doc moved in with them. He lived with them (and their seven children) the rest of his life. He was a bachelor, round, rather jolly, lovable, sparse with words. He used to give the family children silver dollars for Christmas. He worked for the church. Among other duties, he rang the bells announcing Mass. At one time, I was told, he had a popcorn wagon that he presided over on the downtown streets of our town. But that was well before my time.

Facing the house from the sidewalk, we first lived on the right side, then remodeled and moved to the left side. When I was about twelve, we rented the right side to my uncle Bob, his wife, Red, and their daughter. Several years later, we—my parents, my two brothers and I (my older sister had married)—moved to the house my parents had built on seven acres a mile or so outside of town.

While my uncle Bob and his family were living next door, their dog, Tony, was hit and killed by a car passing on the street in front of the house. I can still hear Red screaming, "Tony!" as she ran out of the house to the street. That memory was the moment of inspiration for my novel *A Windless Place*.

My parents, although always strapped for money, had good taste and bought only the best, the highest-quality goods. Our homes on both sides of the house were tastefully furnished. The living room carpet was a thick blue and ivory wool with an outsize flower pattern. As a child, I wrestled with my father on that carpet. The furniture was good quality, some of it—including an intricate oak hutch—made by my father in his basement workshop. I always liked the smell of that workshop. Wood shavings smell wonderful. The kitchens were cheerfully decorated—mostly red and yellow, which I still like in the kitchen. The pictures on the wall were reproductions but carefully chosen. On both sides of the house, there was a Franklin stove attached to the original chimney. In both homes, there was an air of warmth, hospitality, and coziness. My parents had personal problems, but our homes—all three of them—were gracious, comfortable, each in its way and for its time in my life.

The house my parents built outside of our small town was beautiful from any objective perspective. We called it "Windy Knoll." The road leading up to the entrance curved around the side of the house and up the hill to a cleared, flat area of about an acre, with evergreen trees (planted by my father) edging the road, a picnic bench (made by my father), a spacious lawn, woods on two sides of the property. There was a creek at the bottom of the hillside that wrapped around the woods and marked the property line. My parents bought the property from a friend who owned a similarly wooded but uninhabited property on the other side of the creek.

At the far end of the knoll was a little shack—the first edifice built on the property when my parents purchased it some twenty years earlier. Near the shack, nestled into the hill, was a one-room concrete-block cottage, a temporary dwelling built while the house was being planned and constructed. Inside the cottage were a few furnishings and a wood-burning stove. I baked a pie or two in that stove.

The entrance to the house was at the top of the knoll facing the lawn and the woods beyond. The entranceway led directly to the main room of the house, which combined living room, dining room, and kitchen. Facing the living room and open to view from all sides was a huge floor-to-ceiling fireplace that extended down to the lower level. A picture window dominated the living room, with windows surrounding the main level.

It was my parents' dream home. They participated fully in the design of it (the architect was a friend of theirs); they watched (from the cottage) as it became a reality; they lived in it for twenty years or so. Then they sold it, not having the means to maintain it, for a dismally low sum, and moved to a small, gray-painted house on a street of like houses in the perpetual gray of Lorain, a town of steel mills and shipyards. There, in that small gray house, they again painted and tastefully redecorated, inside and out, built a tiny shack in the back yard with a pint-sized Franklin stove—the stove duplicated in the attached garage for those occasions when it was too cold or too inconvenient to venture out into the back yard. After enclosing the long back lawn with cedar fencing, the yard—punctuated by bushes, trees, and an old-growth maple—became a haven for wildlife and assorted wild and tame guests. My father built a grapevine arbor just outside the enclosed back porch. He planted flowers, hung bird feeders, installed a bird bath, arranged outdoor seating. As always, my mother presided over the inside space that was her domain. They spent some years in the late-in-life home they had created.

After my mother died—of a massive heart attack—my father lived on in that small house with the long back yard. He loved beauty and nature; he loved my mother because of her beauty and her nature. They made their homes beautiful; they lived in relative disharmony for more than fifty years; they died, ten years apart—my mother suddenly, acutely; my father from two successive strokes. Their hearts gave way, my mother's first—perhaps because she usually gave way first. My father clung to life, to beauty, to nature, but he too had to give way at last, to leave behind what he most believed in.

They were both brought up in devout Catholic families (on both sides four boys, three girls), but ...

My mother was a believer. My father was, at heart, a hedonist, whose pleasures were fixed in this life. I don't believe the promise of paradise ever captured his spirit or his imagination. He loved a beautiful face (especially my mother's), a beautiful flower, a beautiful sunset.

And now it is past 3:00 p.m. I have observed, in silence, without outside interruption or interference, those three solemn Holy Week hours when Christ hung on the cross.

April 11, 2020

The single most important factor in winning the election in November is the ability of every American to vote. The president doesn't want mail-in ballots because, he says, the Republicans will lose with mail-in ballots. That's the way his dysfunctional mind works. There's widespread voter suppression in this country, and the Democrats are the voters being suppressed. There's a great deal of gerrymandering, and Republicans are behind most of it. Despite the president's devastating failure in every aspect of his office, despite being impeached, he could win the election. The prospect of four more years in his shadow is unthinkable.

I listened to Governor Cuomo's news briefing again this morning. He quoted Winston Churchill's 1942 victory speech: "This is not the end. It is not even the beginning of the end. But it is, perhaps, the end of the beginning." Following his briefing, a news analyst spoke of the "humanity" of his conferences.

⌣

A news story today asserted that Americans most likely to be infected by Covid-19 were the faithful, the jailed, and the old.

I am not among the faithful. I am not jailed. I am the old. I have a "preexisting condition" of the heart—as did my parents before me. A physician once told me that virtually everyone has a predisposition for either cancer or heart disease. If we live long enough, he said, we'll find out which one awaits us.

Unlike most of those who are sheltering in place, I don't find my enforced solitude so much a punishment as an opportunity. I have my dog. I have food. I have my writing. I am connected with family and friends. I have my To Do list. If these were "normal" times, I would be living under similar conditions, except that I would be going out and about; I would be with my family and friends; I would be doing my own shopping; I would be going to social events; I would have choices that, temporarily, I've set aside.

On this Holy Saturday, I am hoping to be still, to be focused, to await the resurrection. At some point in the future—but not coinciding with the Easter Sunday Resurrection—there will be a "resurrection" of sorts. We will not be as we were. Perhaps we'll be better. We will, in any event, be transformed.

April 12, 2020

Years ago, I read Evelyn Waugh's novel *Brideshead Revisited*. I'm now watching the television series (first watched, years ago, on PBS). At that time, William F. Buckley hosted, and discussed the Catholic religion (upon which the novel hinges) at great length and with a somewhat overwhelming punditry.

In one scene, at an evening gathering, Lady Marchmain is reading one of G. K. Chesterton's Father Brown mysteries to her family. Just before her son, Sebastian, enters the room, she reads the passage in which Father Brown discusses catching a villain "with an unseen hook and an invisible line." The line, he explained, is long enough for the villain to wander "to the ends of the world," and to bring him back "with a twitch upon the thread."

Lady Marchmain carefully marks the place, then closes the book, as a drunk, reluctant, and unrepentant Sebastian opens the door and joins the family.

A twitch upon the thread

This quote has always stayed with me. It's evocative, both in terms of the story and in terms of religion.

As the novel and subsequent dramatic series make painfully clear, those of us who have been brought up Catholic can never completely escape its gravitational pull. Sebastian spends his young life attempting to escape his mother and her religion, but "with a twitch upon the thread" he is pulled back, again and again, into the mire of her destructive, alienating society.

My attachment to Catholicism has been, if not similar, at least comparable. I have embraced it, then run away from it, again and again. Then, "with a twitch upon the thread," I have come back. Am I again feeling that twitch? Perhaps. Religion, belief, the spiritual, is on my mind, in my thoughts, especially in the last few days.

Here's how I remember the "Nicene Creed," recited in every Mass, and referenced, in part, in Chapter 16 of *A Windless Place*:

I believe in one God, the Father Almighty, Maker of heaven and earth, and of all things visible and invisible. And I believe in one Lord Jesus Christ, the Only Begotten Son of God. Born of the Father before all ages. God of God; Light of Light; true God of true God; begotten, not made, of one substance with the Father; by whom all things were made; who for us men and for our salvation came down from heaven, was born of the Virgin Mary, and was made man; for our sake he was crucified under Pontius Pilate, suffered death and was buried; and on the third day he rose again, in accordance with the Scriptures. He ascended into heaven and is seated at the right hand of the Father. He will come again in glory to judge the living and the dead, and his kingdom will have no end. And I believe in the Holy Spirit, the Lord and Giver of Life, who proceeds from the Father and the Son; who together with the Father and the Son is adored and glorified; who has spoken through the prophets. And I believe in One, Holy, Catholic and Apostolic Church; I confess one Baptism for the forgiveness of sins, And I look for the resurrection of the dead. And the life of the world to come. Amen.

This complete statement of belief was first adopted in 325 AD. It's part of me, part of my psyche. It is with me today, on Easter Sunday, in the Year of the Plague 2020. It is embedded in my past. As Charles Ryder, the narrator of *Brideshead Revisited*, says at one point: "We possess nothing certainly except the past."

April 14, 2020

If I am a believer, then it follows that God, maker of heaven and earth, who made "all things visible and invisible," brought down upon us the plague that is now invisibly ravaging the world. It may have originated in late 2019 at a live animal market in Wuhan, China, but it came from God. Covid-19 came from God.

My belief does not take me there. Covid-19 came from a live animal market in Wuhan, China, not from God. I believe in free will. If God exists outside of the soul, he is not the vindictive God of the Old Testament. His job—in the infinite unknown past—was to enable the existence of the world, the universe. That's it. We do the rest. We are in charge of our destinies—and that is the subject of all life, all civilizations, all history, all story.

For me, story is our gateway to understanding both the world and each other. It is integral to civilization, and it takes many forms: physically, orally, visually or musically rendered, as well as with narrative or poetry. It is our differentiator. Without it, we are pure instinct; we are animals in the best sense—as animal life is predatory but innocent. There are no sinners in the animal world. There is no conscious cruelty. There is survival. In rising up as a biped, in utilizing our arms and our opposing thumbs; in building fires, constructing shelters, forging weapons, consciously planting seeds, we distinguished ourselves from other animals. But it was when we began to communicate with each other beyond the inherent musical tones of any given species that we became human. It was when we began to tell stories that we linked ourselves with the Divine, that the Divine emerged as a possibility.

⌒

Haiku

Here are the rules: 3 lines; 17 syllables divided as follows: 5/7/5.

Going to the store
Buying what I do not need
Pre-pandemic treat.

April 16, 2020

Today I will offer up my statistics to the 2020 Census. I've been putting it off, as I've been putting off my 2019 tax preparation. It's time for both.

It's late morning. The sky is blue. The April sun—so different from the glare of summer—is inviting. The air is cool, with a light breeze lifting the leaves ever so gently. Neighbors pass at intervals, wearing masks (now required in my area whenever anyone leaves the house).

My mail for the last week or so is unopened. It's in a Trader Joe's bag, awaiting the evaporation of any clinging viral poison. I will open it all at once, discarding the envelopes. I have not been inside my car since March 13. I wonder if it will start. It has never not started. Indi is asleep in her crate (the door long since removed) in the bedroom, having had her turn in the yard and been fed, knowing I will be at my desk for some hours. She chooses either her crate (her "cave") in the bedroom or her oval bed in the living room. Sometimes at night I throw a sheet over my bed covers and bring her up on the bed with me. She sleeps, almost unmoving, as long as I do, close against me. We comfort each other.

I am increasingly grateful for my life, for the start of each day, for that first cup of coffee—hot, black, organic breakfast blend—for the morning hours of writing, meditating, organizing. I'm grateful that my nine-year-old MacBook Pro still starts or restarts when I sit down at my desk. I'm grateful for my iPhone, which connects me to the news, to MSNBC, to Messages, to my Mac mail (especially when my laptop is sluggish).

I'm grateful for my small, quiet residence, the fenced-in yard (locked against the gardeners for some weeks now), the food in my refrigerator and cupboards, the clean water that pours out of my faucets, the flame that starts up when I turn on my gas stove. I'm grateful for every family member, every friend, every bird shouting its delight in the season, for the fresh—deceptively fresh—air, the mild days, the blissfully chilly nights. I'm grateful for the gift I've been given of a long life. I pray to the God within me or beyond my understanding that I will live long enough to see my fourth novel published next year, and then a fifth novel, and a sixth; that I will live long enough to see my grandsons grow up and my son and daughter-in-law grow older. It's not so bad to be old. It's infinitely better than not to be at all.

April 17, 2020

The population of the United States is about 327 million. Our Covid-19 testing, I heard today, is at one percent. The infectious numbers keep going up—at midday U.S. confirmed cases 884,054; U.S. deaths 35,878—but the testing statistic is stuck at one percent.

The president will not budge. Although his power is "total," he insists the responsibility is with each individual state. Governor Cuomo responded with an eleven-minute rant during his press briefing today, but nothing will change. Trump is incapable of change, no matter how many of our fellow Americans die.

There is more and more news about nursing home deaths, which, to date, have not been well tracked. Nursing home deaths have soared. Moms and Dads, Grandmas and Grandpas, are dying in droves in close quarters within the walls of these residences, many of which are privately owned and for which the numbers are not available.

~

A random headline that I scanned during the noon hour today noted that, after more than 200 days in orbit, our space station crew returned "to a changed Earth"; changed, in that a global pandemic has invisibly transformed our planet into something strange and unfamiliar.

Although its message is ominous, I'm intrigued by what, for me, that headline conveys, which is: Having been in space for 200 days, our space station crew lands on planet Earth, and Earth is as wondrous a place as when Apollo 11's Eagle lunar module made its moon landing on July 20, 1969, and astronauts Neil Armstrong and Buzz Aldrin walked on its surface.

~

I was in Paris, with my lover, on July 20, 1969, when humans first walked on the moon. We rented a car in Paris and made our way south, staying at a different chateau each night. Our two-week getaway was a modest success, and our only extended vacation. I was moody—ups and downs that I inflicted on both of us. I touched on it in a story I wrote called "The Round Room."

I was sensitive to the perception of us as a couple. I'm sure no one (especially the French) cared that I had to show my passport at each place we stayed, but I cared. I could never quite escape my background, my religion, my conscience. I wanted to ignore it and enjoy this once-in-a-lifetime trip with my lover, but I couldn't—not quite. So I lashed out—at him. But that was only some of the time. There were moments, hours, of bliss in being with him, in being in France, in being in the intimacy of a small, foreign car as we sped along French roads and through French villages, with much wine and good food for dinner, and lovemaking in our room in an ancient chateau.

In my life, I've only been to five foreign countries: Canada (in my youth and as an adult), England, Scotland, and France (in my traveling twenties), and India (in my yoga forties). I am relatively untraveled although, on my second trip to England, I stayed for nearly six months, and I was two months in India. I was, therefore, a "traveler," not a "tourist," as a character says in Paul Bowles's *The Sheltering Sky*.

My first trip to England, with a friend and work associate, was three weeks long, in the supremely lovely, uniquely "British" months of April and May. My second trip was my six-month stay, mostly in a rented room in Chelsea, where I wrote *Willa*, my first (unpublished) novel. My third trip was with my lover, after our flight from New York to London. We stayed at the Cavendish Hotel before moving on to Paris and those two weeks of (semi) bliss. The Cavendish was my first experience with the "passport" stare. I felt the eyes of the world on me. How little it mattered. How little anyone cared. But I was young, and I had not yet thrown off—obviously, have never completely cast off—the fetters of Catholicism.

April 18, 2020

The Times Literary Supplement reported yesterday: "It is a truth universally acknowledged that women read more fiction than men." An appropriate take on that famous quote, since it was as true in Jane Austen's day as it is now. In a book review of *Why Women Read Fiction: The Stories of Our Lives*, by Helen Taylor, we're told that women account for 80 percent of fiction sales in the UK, the US, and Canada. However, at least in the review, the "why" is vague and ultimately unsatisfactory. So I'll take a stab at it.

Women read more fiction than men because, for women, it brings pleasure and has no negative implications. Many men still, in our time, have a highly sensitive, easily punctured, sense of their own masculinity. Reading nonfiction is an acceptable use of a man's time; reading fiction or poetry is not. There it is. It is a cultural given, and it seems not to have changed in the centuries in which we've had what we describe as fiction—whether we elect as the first novel *The Tale of Genji*, written by a noblewoman named Murasaki Shikibu in the early 11th century; the 17th-century *Don Quixote* by Miguel de Cervantes; or *Robinson Crusoe* by Daniel Defoe, written in the 18th century.

Note that two out of three of those first authors were men. Men are able to write fiction with no attendant reflection on their masculinity; it is the reading of fiction that sprouts the embarrassing blemish.

More importantly, fiction did not begin in the 11th century, or the 17th or 18th centuries. It began with the *Iliad* and the *Odyssey*, in the cultural abundance of Greek and Roman societies. It began before that, with the Sanskrit epics *Ramayana* and *Mahabharata*. It began long before that, with a small group of men and women sitting in the warming glow of an evening fire, regaling each other with stories they had heard, or pretended they had heard, of hunting, heroism, courage, sacrifice—and love.

It began with story, and story began with language itself.

So I take exception to the notion that women are the fiction readers of our time, and of past times. Every one of us, male and female, without exception, loves a good story; every one of us, without exception, finds a way to enjoy a good story—whether it's between the pages of a book or in gossip, or in the bawdy words of a man dressing up an anecdote with fictional detail for the entertainment of three or four of his fishing buddies. Our lives are filled with story. Our lives would be empty, vacuous, without story.

Story is everywhere. We lasso our lives with fiction—but there are multitudes of wild ponies out there on the hills and prairies of our lives that we manage to tame in other ways, with words divine and profane, whether or not they are captured between the pages of a book.

April 20, 2020

Yesterday I went grocery shopping—online. The app is called Instacart. Delivery (based on my choice) is Thursday morning, April 23. The last time I grocery shopped was on March 27, when my daughter-in-law was my delivery person. Now, it seems, many of us are opting for delivery, versus going out into this dangerous world.

Coronavirus numbers update:

Global cases: more than 2.4 million
Global deaths: at least 168,500

US cases: more than 766,600
US deaths: at least 40,931

To which I'll add:

US nursing home deaths: more than 7,000

To which I'll also add that, after gathering these statistics, I did something I've done a couple of times before during this period in our collective lives—I got into bed and pulled the covers over my head. Not the best solution, but it seemed to help, as it has done before. I got up, somewhat refreshed, and managed to get myself through the rest of the day.

April 21, 2020

Global cases: 2,500,156
Global deaths: 171,810

US cases: 800,932
US deaths: 43,006

To which I'll add:

California cases: 33,879
California deaths: 1,225

Los Angeles County cases: 13,816
Los Angeles County deaths: 617

I can't do this every day. I can only manage a periodic look at the statistics, in which the numbers are still going up. Perhaps I'll look again when the numbers start to go down—but when will that be? Some of the statistics are starting to include recovered cases; that's a good sign.

April 24, 2020

"But are we good?"

Louise looked at the faces of her friends. Her three friends looked back at her, each evenly divided by the Zoom screen.

Charlie's expression was, as usual, wry but good-humored.

"If we're good," he said, "*when* we're good—it's because of personal, family, or societal pressure."

His voice was amicable, as though presenting an evident fact.

"By personal pressure, you're referring to our conscience?" said Louise.

"Our conscience, as nurtured by family and society," Charlie replied, his even white teeth revealed between stubble of a moustache above, brief, gray-infused stubble of a beard below.

"I want to do the right thing," said Theresa. "I don't have to struggle with my conscience to know that."

"*I* do," said Sybil. "I'm selfish. I struggle with my conscience all the time."

Louise loved Sybil's transparency, always refreshing in a group hampered by the reservations of an older generation. Not yet forty, and bolstered by social media, Sybil believed it was "healthy" to live one's life as though it were an open book or—in contemporary terms—an ongoing video diary.

"I feel as though I'm losing my center, my soul," said Louise.

She looked at the computer screen, waiting for a response to the distress she was trying to express.

⌒

Although they called themselves a book club, the four friends were bound together by much more than the books they read and discussed. Coming together by chance, at a Meetup book club in Los Angeles, they had splintered off and merged into a tight group over the course of ten years and a hundred discussions that usually veered into the personal, the topical, and the philosophical.

They met, periodically, at each other's homes, to talk and to sample an endless supply of evening refreshments that ranged from sushi to thick, wintry soups. Now, isolated by the pandemic, they were meeting online.

Sybil had initiated the idea of virtual book club meetings, after the shelter-in-place order spread across the country. This was their second virtual meeting, following a bumpy start and technical glitches the previous month.

Although Louise had suggested that they discuss Daniel Defoe's *A Journal of the Plague Year* for this Zoom meeting, she realized she needed to describe her feelings before they discussed the book.

"We're losing a lot of time in the outside world," said Sybil. "A lot of us have lost our jobs. But I don't see how you've come to lose your soul."

"Maybe you just misplaced it," said Charlie.

"Let her talk," said Theresa, in her imperious voice.

Louise took a deep breath. She looked past the faces on the screen to the rooms in the background, pinpointing a familiar bookshelf, a table around which they had gathered, a vase of purple Pacific Coast iris like those she had touched, brought close to her face, in another time, another spring.

"Is it spring?" she said, slowly. "Is it still spring? I feel as though a hundred years have passed since the year began. We've been hurtled into a world of simultaneous isolation and chaos—and there's no way back; sometimes there seems to be no way forward. It's so strange, so unnatural, to have isolation and chaos at the same time. I can escape isolation, but chaos—perhaps death—is the alternative.

"I don't know how to confront the chaos of tens of thousands of deaths in our country alone, in a matter of *weeks*—always creeping up and up—every time I summon the courage to look at the statistics. There are so many who are gone—just like that. Like a light bulb switched off. How can I attach an individual life to each of those who died, give each a name, a family, a job, a potential future that was denied him or her—the way the news does periodically, to remind us that these people lived and breathed and had their beings a few days ago? There's an awful finality to those creeping numbers. How many thousands have died today? How many hundreds of thousands are mourning them?

"So maybe we're not good," Louise concluded. "Maybe we're being punished, in a sort of Biblical sense."

There was silence as the faces on the screen stilled to listen. Then all three spoke at once.

Sybil was the first to make herself heard, as she sat in her sunny country-style kitchen, in her gracious Pasadena house, matching stainless steel sink, refrigerator, range dominating the back wall, iPad tablet roosting above the sink, readily available for recipes or FaceTime. She was the second wife of a well-to-do Pasadena physician.

"Your soul is intact," said Sybil in a raised voice. "Our souls are intact."

"How do you know?"

Louise was careful to keep her voice curious rather than confrontational.

"Because they're safely housed within us," Sybil replied. "They're not a part of the chaos."

"What about all of those who are dying in the chaos?"

"Each of them died, or is dying, with his or her soul intact. We can't lose our souls—not even to chaos."

Sybil's was often the most optimistic voice, the most comforting, the most soothing—at least to Louise's ears.

"Nothing and nobody is taking away *my* soul," said Theresa. "Just let them try."

Louise laughed along with the others, the computer screen capturing their faces as they relaxed, allowed themselves a moment's accord, a stretch, a yawn, a furtive look around the room, as if to assure themselves that all was as it should be in their separate households.

"I can't follow the news the way I used to," said Sybil. "I have to ration it, just as I ration everything else in my life these days."

"I can't *not* watch it," said Charlie. "I try to get at least five minutes of exercise, an hour of sunshine, and three hours of news a day."

"But why immerse yourself in all that's wrong in the world?"

"There is this basic need I have—to know what's going on outside of my own little orbit."

"But it's so—disheartening."

"Not the sunshine. Otherwise—yes."

Charlie was in his West Hollywood "playroom," as he called it. In the background, against a faux-brick wall, Louise could see two bookshelves carelessly packed with DVDs, CDs, hardbacks, paperbacks, journals. She loved that he was an editor in the film industry, with its alternate reality and opinions. A husband and dad to two small boys by a second marriage—he referred to Sybil as a member of his "second-spouse club"—his wife, Joan, was friendly to the group but seldom seen. The boys, and Fido, their dog, liked to interrupt him when he was online—to the delight of Sybil and Louise, the annoyance of Theresa.

"Let's get back to the book," said Theresa.

Theresa could be counted on to keep them on topic. The tendency of the group was to have a grand, all-encompassing discussion—but Theresa was quick to remind them that they were a book club, come together to discuss a book they were reading or had read.

Louise respected Theresa for her sharp mind and well-considered opinions. She was tidy in her ways, terse in her comments, willing to listen but not one to capitulate once she had formed an opinion. Like Theresa herself, her Echo Park home—hers alone since her husband, Turk, had died—reflected her neat, incisive mind and her precise, indisputable taste for the traditional.

"I'll read the first paragraph," said Theresa.

It was about the beginning of September, 1664, that I, among the rest of my neighbours, heard in ordinary discourse that the plague was returned again in Holland; for it had been very violent there, and particularly at Amsterdam and Rotterdam, in the year 1663, whither, they say, it was brought, some said from Italy, others from the Levant, among some goods which were brought home by their Turkey fleet; others said it was brought from Candia; others from Cyprus. It mattered not from whence it came; but all agreed it was come into Holland again.

"Sounds familiar," said Charlie. "I could swear I heard something like that on the news recently."

"A couple of months ago at most," said Sybil.

"Let's see," said Theresa. "I'm going to change a few proper nouns and read it again."

It was about the beginning of January, 2020, that I, among the rest of my neighbours, heard in ordinary discourse that the plague was returned again in China, and particularly at Wuhan, towards the close of the year 2019, whither, they say, it was brought, some said from a live animal market, others from a lab, among some passengers that were brought home by air to the West Coast; others on the East Coast said it was brought from Spain; others from Italy. It mattered not from whence it came; but all agreed it was come into the country again.

"We won't fact-check at this point," said Theresa. "I merely wanted to make a point."

"Yes," said Louise, "Your point is well taken, and I agree with our book choice—especially since I was the one to suggest it. Defoe's *Journal* is relevant, even though it refers to an event that happened more than 350 years ago."

"And has happened multiple times before and since—notably 1918–1920," said Theresa.

"In much the same way," said Sybil.

"Why?" said Louise. "Why has it happened in much the same way, over and over again? Why can't we learn from the past?"

"Churchill said it as well as anybody," said Charlie. "Those who fail to learn from history are condemned to repeat it."

"He, along with a number of other historians," said Louise. "If we're condemned to repeat our blunders, our wrongdoing, over and over again, then we're *not* good."

"Depends on how you define 'good,' said Charlie. "We can be misguided and still be good."

"I want to believe that," said Louise.

"Going back to the book," said Theresa, "let's discuss."

"It takes a certain stamina to read this book," said Sybil. "It goes on and on, relentlessly, without a break, to the very end."

"It's the nature of the subject," replied Theresa, "and it's the way Defoe writes."

"We'll choose something more to your taste next time," said Charlie. "We don't want to depress our Sybil."

"Thanks, Charlie," said Sybil. "I'll eat my next batch of chocolate chip cookies in your honor."

"Jesus, I miss those cookies," said Charlie, stroking his stubble. "I miss your kitchen. I miss you."

"I agree with Sybil," said Louise. "It's not an easy read. I can relate to so much that sounds contemporary—but it's obviously another time, another culture, where surgeons are 'chirurgeons,' and 'dog killers' are appointed to rid the town of dogs—40,000 of them, we're told. Cats are also forbidden, but apparently they were smart enough to make themselves scarce. Dogs have no sense when it comes to family loyalty."

There were grunts and chuckles from the Zoom faces. Louise and Charlie were dog lovers, although Louise's dog, Jack, had died the previous year. Theresa had two majestically aloof cats. Sybil had chosen a spotless home over pet ownership.

"What do we want to take away from this reading?" said Theresa, intent on bringing them back to topic.

"Here's my takeaway," said Louise. "We are, perhaps, good at our core, but we don't learn from the past; we make the same mistakes again and again. Every generation, it seems, starts over again from scratch, forgetting or not acknowledging all that came before. Does that make us good or bad, moral or amoral, wise or stupid, intelligent or hopelessly block-headed?"

Louise glanced outside while she waited for the response. Between crowded bookshelves, a double-hung casement window looked out onto her patio, brilliant pink bougainvillea crowding the trellis next to the window, pushing against the screen. Divorced many years since, she lived comfortably on her own in a small bungalow in Silver Lake.

"I'll vote for block-headed," said Charlie.

"I believe the good, the decent, our fellow feeling for each other, will surface, will dominate in the long run," said Sybil, adding, almost in a whisper, "even if evil sometimes prevails."

"We are what we have always been," Theresa said. "We don't change from generation to generation. We learn, we make great gains in science and technology, we make inroads for social equality, but we are at heart tragically flawed. We will, it seems, revert to tyranny, suppression, nationalism, tribalism, if pushed hard enough—perhaps by something as big as a global pandemic."

The four friends were quiet, contemplative. When Louise spoke again, she was looking away from the camera eye, away from her friends, her eyes again focused on the bougainvillea. She spoke softly.

"So," she said, "what you're saying is, we're not hopeless— but, for the most part, we're *not* good."

April 28, 2020

I read an article today about how we will remember—or not remember—this pandemic. The gist of the article is that we will not remember much of what we're experiencing during this time. The days, and what we do in the course of those days, will merge together. We'll remember key emotional moments, but not the experience in its daily details. I believe this, intrinsically, which is why I'm keeping this journal, and becoming obsessive about recording what I do each day, from the most trivial details—perhaps a note about what I had for dinner—to my inmost feelings, which become a part of this journal in one way or another—as journal entry, memoir, essay, fiction, news commentary, the occasional haiku.

I want to remember. This time can't just become a blur of days, routine, anxiety, some level of family comfort, some level of discipline and/or inspiration to keep me writing. I want to remember details: what did I do, who did I talk to, what did I write, what did I think, what did I feel? I can only *report* on what is happening in the rest of the world—with my family, my friends, my community, my state, my country, my world. I have no control over that silent, invisible virus stalking us around the globe; I do have some control over my personal, emotional response to the pandemic. This is what I want to remember.

Sadly, one of the things we will remember are special events we will miss: birthdays, weddings, funerals, holiday gatherings, family reunions, vacations, road trips, shop-till-you-drop days, parties, dinners for two—or twelve.

When was the last time we left our homes with a feeling of freedom overriding feelings of concern, apprehension? For me, it was prior to Friday, the 13th of March.

When was it we first realized that our lives had changed profoundly? What was the inciting incident? For me, it was April 1, when I realized and wrote about my conviction that our lives would never again be the same.

⌒

Today, in the USA, we surpassed the death toll of 58,220 Americans who lost their lives in the Vietnam War, which lasted almost 20 years. Coronavirus deaths as of today: 58,710.

Today, in the USA, we surpassed one million confirmed coronavirus cases among Americans. Confirmed coronavirus cases: 1,031,575.

Today, worldwide, there are 3,131,659 confirmed cases of coronavirus and 217, 203 deaths.

Doing some quick calculations, I come up with a USA toll of 29 percent of coronavirus deaths worldwide; 33 percent of confirmed cases.

Because those sad numbers change so frequently, I feel obliged to enter the time of day: 4:00 p.m. PT, and to record one tragic news story that I just read about, of a New York-Presbyterian emergency room physician, Dr. Lorna M. Breen, who took her own life.

What made her life unbearable? She contracted the virus and survived it. She was 49, a relatively young woman. What were her days like—the stress, the anxiety, the helplessness, the hopelessness, the exhaustion? Her whole adult life dedicated to healing, and then encountering, day after day, those cases that could not be helped, could not be healed. Then, her own sickness and healing. Then—whatever came next, to push her beyond the point where she could continue. How unimaginable her suffering. I weep for her. She said, according to her sister, "I just couldn't help enough people."

⌒

Despite his affable stutter, which is often perceived as hesitancy, Joe Biden is and has been from the beginning my choice for president—but where is he? I see and hear Andrew Cuomo every day. I can find frequent briefings from Gavin Newsom, and certain other prominent governors. I regularly see Speaker Nancy Pelosi and Adam Schiff, my representative, commenting on the Washington scene. I listen to an ongoing parade of political analysts and medical experts. But where is VP Joe Biden? He makes an appearance from his basement office periodically, for an interview, or when he has been endorsed by another prominent politician—today by Hillary Clinton. Otherwise, he seems to recede into the background, like our day-to-day memories of this strange time-out-of-time in our lives.

He should be out there, every single day. We should see and hear from him, every single day. He cannot become a nonentity even before he's formally given the Democratic presidential nod. What are his strategists thinking? What are they planning? Bring him forward. I want to tune into his narrative every single day, as I do that of Andrew Cuomo. I feel as though I have come to know Governor Cuomo, in terms of his politics and his personal life. He never fails to narrate a personal story during the course of his briefing. Today, he talked about his grandfather, a poor immigrant "ditch digger" who managed to open a neighborhood grocery store, who fed his neighbors and customers during the Depression.

I know, from my reading of news and analysis, that Andrew Cuomo made a lot of mistakes, missed critical opportunities for clamping down on his state and ultimately saving lives. But my inclination is to understand, to forgive, because he is such a real and immediate presence in the world I'm observing right now. He is clear, factual, humorous, genuine.

So, where is Joe Biden? He needs to show his face, broadcast his message, win me over, every single day between now and Tuesday, November 3. Trump is out there wherever we look or listen—the cartoonish orange of his fake hair and bottle-tanned skin, his babyish features and round "O" of a mouth, his extra-long red tie, his syrupy voice. His shout-out of a name is everywhere, in almost every news headline. If all publicity is good, he has already won reelection. No matter how outrageous, Trump is news, dominating the headlines— while Joe Biden meets with his strategists and public health experts in his basement office—and we wait for him to emerge.

April 29, 2020

"Presidents have overwhelming power these days."

Michael Beschloss, author and presidential historian, made this comment on MSNBC today, citing a failure within the Constitution itself.

In other words, we have no weapon except for our vote, which may very well be denied to significant portions of the population because of voter purging, gerrymandering, and denial of our right to vote by mail.

⌒

In a Chuck Todd interview this morning on MSNBC, a physician is worried about the balance between being *passionate* about his mission and his work, and being *dispassionate*, in order to do what he has to do.

I love this philosophical conundrum. It is a wonderful metaphor for the medical profession and for what they're being forced to deal with on a day-to-day basis, as well as a thought-provoking question for all of us who hope to be inspired, as well as orderly and disciplined, in pursuing our creative lives.

⌒

"We must act now. If we do not, history will cast its verdict with those terrible, chilling words—too late."

Those were the words of Winston Churchill in 1939, as he tried to convince Parliament that Germany posed a major military and existential threat to the world. The words struck me this evening, as I watched *The Gathering Storm*, a movie about Churchill's efforts to alert his fellow politicians and the world to the approaching threat of war and potential dictatorship.

How fitting those words, in our time, when the war is a raging global pandemic, and an autocrat sits in the White

House, wearing no clothes—as is evident to anyone willing to believe what they see with their own eyes.

⌒

Meanwhile, life—along with its guilty pleasures—goes on.

I just read that, in Belgium, everybody is being encouraged to eat more fries in order to utilize an excess of more than 750,000 tons of potatoes—as restaurants and other major buyers cut back during the global pandemic.

May 2, 2020

I had a FaceTime conversation today with my nephew about how many of his friends and work associates in Ohio perceive the pandemic—as opposed to how he and I see it. He pointed out that, for many of them, belief in God, in the soul, in that which is a concept—an article of faith rather than a tangible object—is no longer relevant, no longer part of their lives. For that reason, he surmises, the pandemic does not exist for them in a real way. "If they can't see it," he said, "it doesn't exist."

This is an extraordinary thought—but a wise observation. Why are protesters, carrying firearms, threatening Michigan's Governor Gretchen Whitmer, demanding an end to the lockdown? Why are sun lovers flocking to beaches in California, Texas, Georgia, Florida? Why are men and women flaunting the guidelines for gathering in restaurants and other public places? The answer is obvious: It may happen to other people, but it won't happen to me. It's all hype. It's all politics. I have the right to go back to my job and, incidentally, to bear arms. I have the right to walk on the beach. I have the right to live and/or die as I damn well please. No scientist, no fucking politician, is going to tell me what to do and when to do it.

May 3, 2020

I dreamed I was out in a community of people, in a crowd, by myself, and I realized I was not wearing a mask. I stopped at a hotel to see if I could beg or borrow a mask. A young man who worked in the hotel, at the risk of his job, said he would try to give me a mask. He pulled out, from a store of goods, a pile of supplies meant for individual guests, each one rolled into a dark towel. He unrolled the towel and gave me a small packet. I opened the packet and inside were two pairs of sunglasses. I put on a pair of sunglasses and I said, "This won't protect my nose and my mouth." He shrugged and said, "That's all I have." I gave the sunglasses back to him and left. I was again among a crowd of people with no protection over my face. I felt very fearful. I tried to get away from the crowd by climbing a set of stone stairs carved into a wall that was about two stories high. The steps were crumbling and too steep for me. Also, I was carrying something—a very long, slender cardboard box—about the right size for long-stemmed roses. A man climbed the stairs behind me and helped me. He took the package from me, then pulled me up the stairs.

I continue to listen to Governor Andrew Cuomo's daily briefings. From him, I get the facts, the science, the projections, the personal, and the philosophical. Today, he said that "reopening" the tri-state region is more of an art form than the closing down and all that preceded it. I like this analogy. For me, it means we have to be creative, disciplined, patient.

This is in stark contrast to "reopening the economy," which is code for fast-tracking the current guidelines for sheltering in place and distancing.

Cuomo also said that the virus that came from Europe to New York was "a different strain of virus" than that which traveled from China to California. Apparently, in its journey through Europe, into Italy and other countries, it morphed into something else, into its own horrific, invisible strain. It's frightening, the thought of a virus not only deadly but capable of changing its identity as it moves from continent to continent. It's almost too frightening to contemplate—which is why some of us in this country refuse to acknowledge its existence. After all, we can't see it or smell it or taste it or touch it or feel it—so how can it exist?

Governor Cuomo inserted one of my favorite quotes into the press briefing:

"Those who don't know history are destined to repeat it."

He attributed it to Edmund Burke (1729–1797), whom he described as "an Irishman."

I have done this search before, and have always come up with several attributions, including Edmund Burke. The others:

George Santayana (1863–1952)
"Those who cannot remember the past are condemned to repeat it."

Winston Churchill (1874–1965)
"Those who fail to learn from history are condemned to repeat it."

My preference is the Churchill interpretation. He had such a way with words.

Governor Philip Murphy of New Jersey was a virtual guest during Cuomo's press briefing. After his report, he signed off with a reference to "the better days ahead." It reminds me of the ironic lyrics of "Happy Days Are Here Again," written in 1929 and popular in the early 1930s, during the depths of the Depression.

We have to look forward. We are geared to look forward, to be optimistic, to be hopeful. No matter what we go through, no matter what happens to us as individuals, within our communities, countries, continents, we will win in "the better days ahead."

I shudder every time I hear a reference to "elevators" in the time of a pandemic, and what might lurk within those small moving boxes as they carry us up and down, down and up. I was stuck in an elevator once, in India, with another visitor from the States, for a very long 20 minutes or so, before a grinning elevator maintenance man released us from a relatively safe height two feet or so from the floor. We both ran out of the building, anxious to be as far away as possible from the source of those agonizing minutes when we were trapped. I've been fearful of elevators since then.

Very different from my current view of elevators as viral traps, where social distancing is impossible, and breathing on and touching one another is inevitable, even with masks and the best of intentions. I'm grateful I'm not living in one of those "dense" population areas, where elevators, mass transit, and other hazards are unavoidable.

May 5, 2020

Haiku

> *Pandemic salute*
> *to May as death soars and we*
> *choose to be heedless.*

The estimate of deaths from the Covid-19 virus has been drastically revised upward: to 250,000 by the end of the year. As "Morning Joe" commented on MSNBC this a.m., we have been "abandoned" by our president. Trump is intent on the economy—his only road to reelection—at the cost of a quarter of a million American lives.

I can't wait for Tuesday, November 3. We need to remove Trump before our population is decimated by his complete relinquishment of responsibility in favor of forcibly reopening the economy.

May 12, 2020

While I was growing up, we had standing rib roast for dinner almost every Sunday. There was always a salad, with lettuce, tomatoes, other seasonal vegetables, and peas. I don't remember having bread, potatoes, or anything starchy. For the rest of the week, dinner was usually modest—ground beef casseroles, chops, chicken—the usual.

For many years now, I've eaten standing rib roast once a year, on Christmas Day. I introduced Yorkshire pudding as an accompaniment following my study of English literature and several trips to England. Yorkshire pudding has become a mainstay, peas are a must, to which we add holiday side dishes and desserts provided by family members and guests.

In my thirties, I discovered yoga. It became my obsession over the next years. I devoured it—taking classes, practicing, reading, studying, traveling to conventions. I lived in Ann Arbor, home to the Palmer family who, in 1956, first brought Mr. B.K.S. Iyengar to the States. My first visit to California was for the 1990 Iyengar Yoga National Convention in San Diego. I studied at the Iyengar Institute in Pune, India, after which I became a Certified Iyengar Yoga Instructor. Which brings me back to the roast beef.

I don't remember exactly when it happened, but I do remember losing my taste for meat as my interest in and practice of yoga developed. It wasn't a sudden, or even a calculated, decision. As my diet became more plant-based, I felt more comfortable with the poses. It was never a sacrifice to give up meat. I just felt better without it.

Over the years, I've found it harder and harder to disengage myself from the animal behind the meat cut—the cow, the pig, the lamb, the turkey, the chicken, the fish. And I wonder about our choice of animals. We don't eat dogs or cats or horses, at least not in this country. I think about the salmon I love to eat on occasion, fighting its way upstream so it can land on my dinner plate. The cow, with its limpid brown eyes and gentle ways, even if a dairy cow, may end its days as standing rib roast or hamburger meat. The caged lamb or calf, whose movements are limited so that it can fatten up, will become lamb chops or veal. They're all the same to me—dogs and pigs, horses and cows. They're sentient creatures. They have skin and bones, flesh and feelings. We have chosen to consume some of them, and to live with others on terms of affection. What age-old instincts drive us? Once in a while, certain wilder species consume us—but that's the exception and, for the most part, not in this part of the world.

But, of course, I see this issue from behind my tinted glasses. Truth be told, I have no problem cooking meat for others—or eating meat once or twice a year. I have never tried to convert a meat-eater. It's a very personal choice. Like growing up with a religion, growing up in a meat-eating family was, for me, a permanent condition, even if recessive. I can back off, evade, avoid, but that fundamental hunger never goes away entirely. I'm a lapsed Catholic and a lapsed meat-eater, but I still, on occasion, miss the Church, the rituals, the sacrificial host—the Sunday feast.

> *Lamb of God, who taketh away the sins of the world,*
> *have mercy on us.*
> *Lamb of God, who taketh away the sins of the world,*
> *have mercy on us.*
> *Lamb of God, who taketh away the sins of the world,*
> *grant us peace.*

⌒

Now, because of Covid-19, meat-processing plants, already end-of-the-road for the animals, have become potentially lethal for the men and women who are forced to work in the plants or lose their livelihoods. Executioner and executed caught in a death trap—one needing the work, the other considered a "necessary" consumer commodity.

If I were not already a vegetarian, I would be tempted to jump off the train at this point.

May 15, 2020

"Vaccine or no vaccine, we're back."

Donald Trump spoke those words today, Friday, at one of his typical politicized coronavirus news updates. Truck drivers honked incessantly in the background, applauding Trump and his back-to-business stance, while Trump announced his "Operation Warp Speed" to develop a vaccine by the end of the year, his latest belated effort to overtake a virus that outdistanced him months ago. Military experts and other sidekicks stood in the background, together with a silent, mask-covered Dr. Anthony Fauci.

Meanwhile, *The Lancet*, in an unsigned editorial, and in no uncertain terms, told the medical community, and the world at large, that the USA needs a new president, pointing out that Americans, come January, must put a president in the White House "who should not be guided by partisan politics."

⌒

"In other news …"

The House of Representatives voted today on a Covid-19 aid package of more than three trillion dollars. The aid package includes a historic "rules" change to allow lawmakers to vote remotely during the pandemic.

May 16, 2020

I have often wondered how to wrap my head around Donald Trump's stupefying and deadly character traits. To say that he's a sociopath seems inadequate—unless we explore a key component of that diagnosis: lack of conscience.

Tony Schwartz, who co-authored Trump's 1987 *Art of the Deal*—but who, in fact, ghostwrote the book—affirmed in an MSNBC interview yesterday that Trump "has no conscience" and "is solely motivated by the need to dominate."

This gives the president "an enormous advantage," Schwartz said, because "Trump doesn't feel or make a distinction between right or wrong" in situations in which most people are "limited" by their respect for truth as well as their concern for others. Trump, it seems, has no inherent limitations imposed by conscience, morality, or society. Schwartz noted that it's hard for us to understand his "absence of conscience" and "absence of empathy"—qualities that are "second nature" to most of us.

"Trump sees the world in terms of winners and losers," Schwartz said, "and he hates losers," including many of the people who vote for him. The "winners," on the other hand, are the dictators he admires: Putin, Kim Jong Un, Erdogan.

The deaths from the coronavirus "don't matter to him," Schwartz concluded. "If it's a decision between saving himself and saving others, it is no contest."

~

"DOA. Dead on arrival."

Trump's words regarding the Coronavirus Relief Bill, passed yesterday by the House of Representatives and headed for the Senate.

May 19, 2020

I feel lonely and overwhelmed. It's not because I have no direction, nothing to do. I have more to do than I can do, comfortably, each day. I've never been without self-direction, the ability to work on my own. I've made my living, except for the few full-time jobs I've had (Cleveland, Chicago, Detroit), providing creative services from a home base or, in Ann Arbor, from my office on South State Street. But …

I've never been by myself for so long—since March—Friday the 13th.

For 65 days, not counting today, I have had no extended face-to-face, body-to-body contact; nor do I regularly walk my dog up and down the streets of my neighborhood; nor do I drive my car. Is this what people do in prison? Shelter in place as they count the days?

It is my own fear that keeps me within the bounds of my home and yard. I sit at my desk every day and watch people walk up and down the street, alone or with their children, with their dogs—without masks. A lot of my neighbors *are* wearing masks—I would put the ratio at about 50:50. But I don't feel comfortable mingling with my neighbors with that ratio confronting me.

I'm also obsessed with the news. I read, listen, and watch the news almost exclusively on my iPhone. I don't need a big screen for news. The big screen is my late-night escape from the distress of my days, when I watch movies, old and new, and dramatic series. Last night I binge-watched *Picnic at Hanging Rock*, a 2018 dramatic series based on Joan Lindsay's 1967 novel and followed by the 1975 feature film. The series was overly long but fascinating.

I can do that. I can stay up till the early hours, sleep in later than I should, because I'm isolated. But I'd rather not. I'd rather be free to come and go as I please, to be with family and friends, to babysit my grandsons, to work part-time as a creative consultant and editor, to quit Instacart and do my own grocery shopping, to walk my dog rather than "running" her in the back yard (she's small and slowing down with age), to eat at a restaurant, to take a day-long road trip to see the spring poppies, to sit close to the ocean and watch the waves wash in, to see *Hamilton* at the Pantages Theater for the second time (as my family and I were scheduled to do on March 29).

The country is reopening—against the death toll, against statistics, against medical and scientific advice, against multiple issues of self-interest and safety. I understand the frustration, the need to return to "normal" life, but I'm not acting on it. I have books to write and publish, a family I want to see mature and flourish, countless small sources of enjoyment and happiness in my day-to-day life. I'm not about to jeopardize any of it. Not now. Not yet. Not, perhaps, for months to come.

May 21, 2020

Statistics today (as compared with April 21)

     Global cases: 5,151,240 (2,500,156)
     Global deaths: 332,299 (171,810)

     U.S. cases: 1,604,843 (800,932)
     U.S. deaths: 95,656 (43,006)

     California cases: 84,057 (33,879)
     California deaths: 3,436 (1,225)

Los Angeles County cases: 40,975 (13,816)
Los Angeles County deaths: 1,976 (617)

May 23, 2020

I'm reading about Trump's move to block travel from Europe, and how it triggered a Covid surge. The summary that follows has been tweaked and reordered, to suit the reader (me).

There were only 3,714 confirmed cases in the United States on March 13, the day European travel restrictions were implemented. Only 176 deaths had been recorded. Those numbers were considered inaccurate because of the scarcity of tests.

After surfacing in China in late December, the contagion had migrated to Europe by early February. Europe, however, did not issue travel restrictions until after the United States had done so.

Trump imposed a partial travel ban from China on January 31, but by mid-February, European strains had been established in New York, where they multiplied and then migrated out to the rest of the country. By March 1, one study indicated, New York probably had more than 10,000 undetected cases, with thousands of additional cases in San Francisco, Chicago, and other cities.

"We closed the front door with the China travel ban," New York's Governor Andrew Cuomo said, "but we left the back door wide open."

It was on March 11 that the World Health Organization declared the coronavirus a global pandemic. That evening, at

9:00 p.m., Trump delivered a European travel block live from the Oval Office, stating, "We will be suspending all travel from Europe to the United States for the next 30 days."

Within hours, experts were warning that it was already too late.

⌒

I went into lockdown on Friday, March 13, and have not yet emerged.

New York, on the other hand, is emerging, with the number of deaths (84) per day under 100 for the first time in two-and-a-half months.

LA County, on the other (other) hand, goes up and up, with 1,032 new cases and 41 deaths since yesterday. No emergence in our immediate future—except for the heedless, the desperate, those exhausted by a long confinement, and optimists who are certain the worst is over.

May 24, 2020

Today's *New York Times* front page is a typographical mass of obituary clips from throughout the country, as we approach 100,000 deaths from Covid-19, which the *Times* describes as "an incalculable loss."

Except for the headline, and a brief intro paragraph, the random list is all that appears on the page. The names, together with a tidbit from their lives, fill the front page and three additional pages—a total of almost 1,000 lives lost and—significantly—only one percent of that fast-approaching, fateful number.

Shades of 9/11, and the very personal obituaries the *Times* ran on those who perished!

We know these people. They are our family members, our friends, our neighbors, our models for loving, useful, and productive lives. Through no fault of their own, they were exposed to a deadly virus, and were swept away. They were here for a reason. Their presence on this earth made our lives better, richer. What *The New York Times* did so well, both today and following the trauma of 9/11, was to transform those deadly statistics into lives that mattered, lives that are missed, lives abruptly cut short.

"None were mere numbers," the *Times* said in its very brief intro. "They were us."

Every remembered life is a one-second short story. Every name helps to make this moment in time click into place. It is a way to bring order to chaos.

What went missing from our lives in the past three months cannot be retrieved. We cannot retrieve those lives, those souls. We can only remember them, as we remember the veterans on this Memorial Day weekend. It seems inadequate, but it's our only shield against loss.

May 25, 2020

For some time, I've been missing the clear plastic top to my sea salt grinder. This morning it occurred to me that I have a plastic bag in a kitchen drawer, into which I put miscellaneous but useful small items, as well as homeless items I can't identify but am reluctant to throw away. There I found the missing part. As I put the top on my grinder and clicked it into place, I felt a sense of satisfaction I have felt before, in other situations, both large and small: *to have kept something for a reason, and to find the reason.* It is, I believe, a need I have to find the missing part, to understand the order of things.

⌒

While I was growing up, my hometown had about 5,000 residents. It was considered, as I recall, a "village" or a "town" rather than a city. Of course, it has grown over the years. These days, my hometown is identified as a "city." Villages or towns grow into cities. It's in the order of things.

What is *not* in the order of things is that fast-approaching number: 100,000 lives lost to Covid-19. It's too late to undo it, but the number of Americans dead from the virus need never have climbed to this astronomical number.

The number dead would have populated 20 towns the size of the hometown I remember. In trying to comprehend the number of dead—all of whom were alive three months ago—I think about populating these 20 towns—perhaps one town in each of 20 states across the country.

Each town would have its own downtown area, its own tree-lined neighborhoods, its own town hall, police and fire stations, schools and churches, its own library. There would be parks and cemeteries, a lumber yard, a grocery store or two, a butcher, a bakery, a drugstore, an ice cream parlor, a recreation center, a bowling alley, a pool hall, a couple of bars, a movie theater—all supported by a few key industries, or by work in nearby cities.

Then, one year, in the course of three months, from late winter to late spring, all 20 of those towns were somehow wiped out, became ghost towns. There were no inhabitants. The inhabitants had disappeared from the face of the earth. They were, in fact, buried beneath the earth—hurriedly, because there were so many to bury—in solitude, because those who grieved for them could not be with them, because no one was allowed entry who did not belong to that particular town.

They had lived, they had thrived, in these 20 small towns. Now they were dead, their houses shut down, their businesses boarded up, their schools and churches empty. Only the cemeteries and crematories were glutted with pressing new business—the business of getting the dead under the ground or transformed into ashes as quickly as possible.

When that was done, when only the shell of each town remained, how would we assess the loss of life, of energy, of aspiration, of joy and connection?

We could not. We cannot. It's like trying to assess the loss of humanity during a world war, during a holocaust, during a nuclear attack, during any disaster fanned and flamed by the hubris, ineptitude, irresponsibility, and indifference of humans. The inhabitants of those 20 towns are gone, but we remain, and the pandemic rages on. It was thrust upon us. We're trapped in its vicious, deadly, chaotic center.

It's not in the order of things.

We're headed for disaster. The news today is disheartening, to say the least. People are crowding together on beaches, at pools, restaurants, shops, boardwalks. Everybody wants to be outside today. Meantime, the only place in the country where the Covid stats are going down instead of up is in the Northeast—Governor Cuomo's territory—and that will change as soon as the barricades are taken down. We might defy the virus, but the virus will persist. It will sweep us away as long as it is potent.

May 26, 2020

Politics is ugly. When combined with a vicious pandemic, the result is chaos. That's what we as a country are experiencing at this moment.

The Memorial Day weekend was a perfect metaphor for the state of our "union." We are a divided nation—divided along overtly political issues—and the only way we can come together as a union again is to rid ourselves of the divisive, unscrupulous man at the top. I am exhausted by my attempts to sift through his digressive tactics, his deceit, his brazen lies. President Tweety (Joe Biden's nickname for Donald Trump) is now threatening to withdraw from the RNC convention in North Carolina if the Democratic governor doesn't agree to a full-fledged 50,000-strong live event.

Today, on MSNBC, Pulitzer-Prize-winning science journalist and author Laurie Garrett said that the pandemic could be a three- or four-year event. That does not seem unimaginable to me. I've always thought of it as a two-year event.

With the current divides and defiance, we could certainly extend the life of the pandemic to its third or fourth birthday.

⌒

Today, in New York's Central Park, a man engaged in bird watching released a video of a confrontation between himself and a young woman who did not have her dog on a leash. When the man politely asked her to leash her dog so that he could continue his activity without disturbance, the woman called 911 and said an African American man was threatening her life. She later apologized, but her hysteria is symptomatic of the deep divide we are experiencing on so many levels, from personal to racial to political.

⌒

I dislike Twitter because it is home base for "President Tweety." I'm grateful I was not induced to open an account when I was creating an author platform. It's frustrating enough for me to go on Facebook periodically. I have to grit my teeth to redirect my website posts from my Facebook Author page. Mark Zuckerberg and Jack Dorsey are being successfully cowed by Tweety. I doubt they'll make any significant moves to block the spread of yet another lethal affliction—a carefully orchestrated barrage of social media disinformation.

I am not a political person. My mother was an ardent Democrat. My father was staunchly apolitical. I've always voted Democratic, although I didn't register as a Democrat until I was middle-aged. I like it when I can keep politics in my peripheral vision. I can't do that now. So much is at stake—more than most of us can fathom. Our very existence is at stake—and this existential threat feeds directly into politics. *It's not manly to wear a mask*, Trump repeatedly implies. Nothing, it seems, will induce the president to wear a mask in public, and so go his cult followers. According to physician and medical reporter Sanjay Gupta, even media personalities like Rush Limbaugh are merely "surrogates" for the president and not important. The buck stops with the cult leader.

I don't want to write about this. I want to write about my memories, my philosophy, my personal history and my history as a writer. Perhaps I'm doing this—even as I complain that I'm being sidetracked by politics, by life interrupted and disrupted—because of the stubborn resistance of people who want only to be free to resume the life they had before March of 2020. I feel their pain, their disbelief, their skepticism, their helplessness.

It's spring. It's a beautiful California day. Everything in me wants to be out and about. What is keeping me back? Only a conviction that what is out there, though invisible, is real and deadly.

May 27, 2020

I was wrong.

Twitter *did* make an attempt to rein in the "hyperactive Twitter troll" in the White House (per columnist Eugene Robinson in *The Washington Post*). Of course, Trump promised immediate revenge, accusing Twitter of interfering in the election, and threatening to "close" social media platforms.

Ha. Why would Trump shut down his favorite spleen outlet? It won't happen. With 80 million followers, in an election year, why would he cut off his own nose to save face?

It's all a ploy. President Tweety is desperate to change the discussion from the only subject that matters to most people—the global pandemic. If he has been able to redirect the thinking of a significant portion of his Twitter followers, he has triumphed—again. He could still win the election.

I'm feeling more like a columnist than a memoirist lately. Enough. I have other things to say and write about.

May 29, 2020

Today, an MSNBC analyst—in the wake of the murder of George Floyd by a police officer in Minneapolis on May 25, and the burning of Minneapolis's Third Precinct by protesters last night—described racial injustice as our country's "original sin."

Trump tweeted that the protesters are "thugs" while, earlier this month, condoning armed protesters at the Michigan statehouse who wanted coronavirus regulations lifted.

May 30, 2020

Good news and bad news today. First, the good news. Elon Musk's SpaceX launched successfully at about 12:30 p.m. PT. It was exciting to watch on my big screen. It brought tears to my eyes. Someone commented, "It's a great moment." It was. Zero to 17,500 MPH in eight-and-a-half minutes. Traveling at five miles per second. A brilliant accomplishment, flawlessly performed.

◡⁓

Then, there's the bad news: A day of protests throughout the country, after the murder of George Floyd, pushed into riot mode by extremists. Minneapolis; Washington, D.C. (outside the White House); Los Angeles; New York. Overnight curfews have been ordered in Atlanta, Chicago, Cleveland, Columbus, Denver, Miami, Milwaukee, Minneapolis, Pittsburgh, Philadelphia, and Portland (OR).

◡⁓

Then, there's the random opinion (mine). It's unlikely that Amy Klobuchar of Minnesota will get the VP pick. Her background as a prosecutor who did not indict policemen accused of violence against African Americans—a group of policemen (according to a report) that included Derek Chauvin—has made her very unpopular with black voters, especially right now, when her record has again come under scrutiny. I hope Joe Biden is paying attention to this. He must make the right pick.

May 31, 2020

"Reading this book is like wading through a quagmire," said Charlie, as he greeted the book club. The four friends were meeting again on Zoom, continuing their discussion of Defoe's *A Journal of the Plague Year*.

"That's probably what it felt like back then, in 1665," said Louise.

Sybil smiled from her frame on the computer screen.

"They seemed to know a lot about *spread*," she said. "They were sheltering in place, keeping their distance, covering their faces in public, avoiding crowds—and getting the hell out of town when things got crazy."

"Very little science and no technology," Louise said, nodding at Sybil, "and they knew as much as we know."

"Except for hand washing," said Theresa.

Charlie resumed his complaint.

"Can we read something a little more stimulating and contemporary next time? Life sucks enough as it is these days."

"What would you suggest, Charlie?" said Louise.

"Just about anything would be an improvement. How about *Plague of Corruption*—about corruption in science— or *A Very Stable Genius*—about our corrupt president?"

"We could plunge into fiction," said Sybil, playfully ignoring his suggestions. "Something more uplifting."

"It *is* a depressing time," said Theresa. "106,000 deaths and counting in our country alone—and so many people acting as though it's over and done with."

"It's not over," said Charlie, "but a lot of people are done with it."

"Including our president," said Sybil.

There was a long pause. The faces framed by the screen were serious, thoughtful.

"Not counting the president, I guess I don't blame people," said Charlie. "I feel trapped. I'm working, and I'm grateful for that, but it doesn't feel right. I'm used to one-on-one, face-to-face collaboration."

"Teaching is what's hard," said Theresa, a retired schoolteacher. "Little kids don't understand what's going on with home schooling, and the bigger kids don't pay attention."

"Sounds like normal kids to me," said Sybil. "Whether the class is real or virtual."

Louise spoke up.

"Meanwhile, back in London, in 1665 …"

"You're right, Louise," Sybil replied. "We're off topic again."

"Who can stay on topic," Charlie said, still edgy, "when the topic is the London plague of 1665? Meanwhile, in present-day USA, people are dropping dead by the thousands, we're having riots in dozens of cities because police are murdering black people, and our cities are being looted and going up in flames."

Louise frowned, carefully modifying her response, not wanting to further irritate Charlie.

"That's exactly why I suggested this book," she said. "We need to look back as well as forward in times like this. By the way, they also had fires in London back then—although it was a year after the plague, and I don't think they were caused by protesters."

"Well, Charlie's right about one thing," said Sybil. "It's hard to focus on an event that happened in another country,

350 years ago, when so much is happening, and changing, right now, right here, from day to day."

"*Have* you read it, Charlie?" asked Louise, politely.

Charlie hesitated before he replied.

"Here and there."

"Let me read a passage," said Louise.

She opened her iPad, scrolled down till she found her place, read slowly and deliberately.

… the plague spread itself with an irresistible fury … it came at last to such violence that the people sat still looking at one another, and seemed abandoned in despair …

She paused and then continued.

… people began to give up themselves to their fears and to think that all regulations and methods were in vain, and that there was nothing to be hoped for but an universal desolation, and it was even in the height of this general despair that it pleased God to stay His hand, and to slacken the fury of the contagion.

Louise gathered her thoughts, wishing she could rest her eyes on the bougainvillea outside her window, take a few deep breaths. But the faces on the screen were waiting for her response to the passage she had just read.

"I keep coming back to some phrases," she said, slowly, "like … 'the plague spread itself with an irresistible fury,' and 'people began to give up themselves to their fears,' to think that 'all regulations and methods were in vain,' that there was 'nothing to be hoped for.'

"That's where we are now. Maybe, for some of us, God will come to our rescue at some point, 'to slacken the fury of the contagion,' but, for many of us, there is no God and no way out of our despair."

"Have you lost all hope, Louise?"

"Not yet, Sybil—but, like Charlie, I'm distressed by the cumulative effect of what has happened, here and around the world, in the past few months."

She studied the faces on the screen, each of whom, over the ten-year life of the book club, she had come to love: Sybil, who wore all of her emotions on the outside; Charlie, who hid his soft underside beneath an outer layer of cynicism; Theresa, who insisted on order and precision—perhaps to cover up her own fears.

Then she spoke again.

"How can our lives have changed so much in so little time? It's a cataclysmic event, like the meteor that wiped out the dinosaurs. Are we the dinosaurs of our era? Is there something different, something better, that will succeed us? We certainly haven't taken care of our home, the planet Earth. We've spent hundreds of years abusing it, polluting it ..."

She took a breath.

"We just launched a spaceship with astounding perfection, but we can't contain our racial hatred here on the ground, in our neighborhoods, in our cities. We pass this hatred along from generation to generation—and *we don't learn*! We don't learn from the past."

"Amen," said Theresa. "Pestilence. Fire. Flood. Maybe we'll survive, but we seem to be headed for a Noah's Ark of a future, a final cleansing."

The other three murmured their assent.

"If there is a God," Louise added, "he's putting out warning signals on all fronts."

Charlie put his hands up in prayer mode and clapped, silently.

"We count on you, Louise, for the philosophical moment. I take your point. I guess I'm just tired. Tired of being restrained. Tired of home schooling my boys, who are tired of being home schooled. Tired of working virtually ..."

"You're one of the lucky ones, Charlie," said Theresa, quick to rebuke. "You've got a job. You're with your family. You're all in good health."

"You're always so fucking right," said Charlie, grinning at Theresa. "Okay, I admit that's just day-to-day grousing, from a guy who's got it pretty good, considering. When I take a look around, I see 40 million or so unemployed, police brutality, a week of protests, fires, looting, a president who blames the media, the mayors, the governors, the far left— anybody except himself—add the fact that nobody knows how much the virus has gotten new legs in the past week or so—and I see we're in a place where that 'irresistible fury' is consuming us—body and soul, you might say. And we're barely into the long, hot summer."

"The fatal breath," Sybil said. She said it forcefully, her frame lighting up as she spoke.

The others looked at Sybil in her Zoom compartment, her pristine kitchen shining in all its whiteness behind her.

"It's a phrase from the book that has stuck in my mind," she said. "I keep thinking about it."

She took a deep breath.

"His last words were, 'I can't breathe.' A police officer handcuffed him, pinned him face down on the street, knelt on his neck ..."

She choked, cleared her throat, tried again.

"Those were his last words ..."

The faces on the screen stilled, waited.

"Don't you see?" Sybil's voice rose. "What we're going through, in the middle of a pandemic, it's ... yes, it's hellish, but it's also inevitable because—we all seem to agree on this—people *don't* learn from the past. Haven't since Adam and Eve. So maybe it's a judgment from God. Maybe it comes from our own brutish behavior. But ..."

She paused, as if waiting for one of the others to speak up. When no one did, she continued, as if stitching her thoughts together as she spoke.

"But it's all *connected*, somehow. There's this contagion that spreads and kills without mercy. And then there's this police officer, almost *relaxed*, one hand in his pocket as he kneels with the full weight of his body on his victim's neck—his face expressionless, without emotion, without even *anger*—as he waits for George Floyd to die ..."

She shuddered.

"Two very different assaults—on our lives, on the very air we breathe. Both impersonal, deadly. It's *connected*—if we can only back off enough to see what's going on."

She held her hands up and, framed bottom left, in her quarter of the Zoom screen, interlocked her fingers in front of her face. She looked very young, the fringe of her short dark hair curling like question marks across her pale forehead.

"There's the virus we can't see, that lives and thrives on the air we breathe—and then there's an innocent man's last cry for mercy—'*I can't breathe.*'"

She squeezed her hands together, hard, then slumped back in her chair.

"Even the contaminated air we breathe was denied him."

June 2, 2020

Why is Donald Trump able to survive and thrive in the polls despite his despicable behavior? Why are Republicans silent, sheepish accomplices? Why isn't there some way to put the brakes on this out-of-control megalomaniac?

What he did yesterday afternoon was detestable. It was the action of a man who has chosen to disregard humanity, Christianity, and the Constitution of our country.

After police had cleared out protesters with tear gas and flash grenades, Trump walked from the White House, flanked by his minions, crossed Lafayette Square, and stood in front of St. John's Church. Holding a Bible (upside down), he told reporters he would "deploy the military" if the protests were not contained.

So. Without warning, shortly before the city's 7:00 p.m. curfew, peaceful protesters across the street from the White House were doused with tear gas and terrified by explosives because the president wanted to have his picture taken holding a Bible at St. John's Church—the "Church of the Presidents."

"On a knife's edge."

A commentator made this remark today, in reference to the tenuous state of our democracy. It immediately brought to my mind the sacred words—not of the Christian Bible Trump so brazenly held up at his photo op in front of St. John's—but of the Upanishads, part of the Hindu scriptures, well remembered from my years of exposure to yoga history, philosophy, and culture.

"The sharp edge of a razor is difficult to pass over; thus the wise say the path to Salvation is hard."

It is also the epigraph of *The Razor's Edge*, W. Somerset Maugham's 1944 novel, a book I've read and reread more than a few times over the years.

⌒

George F. Will published an opinion column in *The Washington Post* a few hours before yesterday's infamous St. John's Church incident, saying "Trump must be removed" and "assume that the worst is yet to come." I admire his prescience.

June 5, 2020

I love what's happening. When I saw images of the huge yellow two-block-long "BLACK LIVES MATTER" slogan painted on the street outside the White House, I felt as though the Washington, D.C., mayor had objectified the frustration of so many of us in a way that is clear, nonviolent, unmistakable—even joyful.

The street was officially renamed "Black Lives Matter Plaza," and the street sign went up today.

Go, you, Mayor Muriel Bowser.

June 8, 2020

Nobody's paying attention. The virus is gaining on us but nobody's focusing on it anymore. People are hitting the streets. Shops and other "nonessential" businesses have reopened. Even in California, bars, gyms, and movie theaters are about to reopen on June 12, as will music, TV, and movie production. But most of all, we're protesting—by the tens of thousands. In cities all over the country—all over the world.

It's as though the pandemic is behind us. Yesterday's news. All that sheltering in place. That tedious stay-at-home mentality. Those frustrating online family calls and business meetings. Over and done with, thank God.

There's a visible remnant: the face mask. It has become a socially acceptable clothing and fashion accessory that many of us are loath to be seen without (except for those who never wore masks in the first place). Sort of a nod to whatever threat might still be out there.

The image of thousands and thousands of people—masked and unmasked—gathered in the streets of dozens of cities is so dramatically opposed to being "alone together" (as one promotion puts it) that I can't quite process it. It's an awe-inspiring response to a hideous murder we all witnessed but, at the same time, it's so out of sync with a global pandemic that it's terrifying. Even though the protests are out of doors, which is supposedly safer than gathering in closed-in spaces, the danger is there in those crowds, hovering everywhere, invisible, deadly.

The fatal breath.

What will be the results? A magnificent display of solidarity, juxtaposed with a cataclysmic, omnipresent plague.

I cannot conceive of a happy outcome.

June 9, 2020

"What's in a name?"

I've often thought of this in connection with African-American surnames—and Rev. Al Sharpton brought it up today, at the George Floyd funeral service in Houston.

"Every time I write my name, I am inscribing history," Rev. Sharpton said in his eulogy.

Rev. Sharpton said that his great-grandfather, Coleman Sharpton, was a slave, and that Coleman Sharpton bore the name of his slave owner, as does every family member who succeeded him.

I looked up the Sharptons' history. The Rev. Al Sharpton's name originated in South Carolina, with slave-owner Alexander Sharpton. Rev. Sharpton's great-grandfather, Coleman Sharpton, was subsequently given "as a gift" to Julia Thurmond, who moved him, along with his wife and two children, to Florida.

Coleman Sharpton was given his freedom at the end of the Civil War.

Julia Thurmond, it turns out, was an ancestor of Strom Thurmond, a prominent states' rights and segregation advocate who ran for the presidency in 1948 on the Dixiecrat ticket. He was a U.S. senator from 1954–2003.

June 11, 2020

I'm lonely.

I've never in my life experienced this level of isolation. Three months of isolation—like a prisoner being punished for unacceptable behavior. The thing is—I have resources. A lot of people have very little to fall back on, in terms of education, work experience, family support. What are those people doing? How are they feeling? Would the protests be as enduring as they have been so far if the alternative were not a continuing state of isolation and frustration combined with joblessness and economic peril?

I can certainly empathize with the feeling of isolation and economic peril. I've done everything I can to cut expenses but—having lost income sources because of the pandemic—I know the panic that lies just beneath the surface. The 12-week total for unemployment, I saw on the news, is 44 million. The Fed Chair—Chair of the Federal Reserve Jerome Powell (a Trump appointee)—says a "significant chunk" of Americans won't get their jobs back. We went from historically low unemployment to an unprecedented high in the space of three months. Another 1.5 million people filed for unemployment this week.

"It's the economy, stupid," is a phrase we've heard many times since James Carville (strategist for Bill Clinton) coined it in 1992. But there's really only one issue, and it's a personal one. It's individuals and families wondering about their financial future.

Meanwhile, back to the plague. After 18 days of continuing nationwide protests—George Floyd's video-captured murder was on Monday, May 25; protests started on Tuesday, May 26—there has been a surge of cases in many states. Is anyone surprised by this development?

A global pandemic continues to rage. Millions of people out of work as we close down the country and shelter in place in an attempt to ward off its fatal breath. Police violence that results in the deliberate murder of George Floyd. A Black Lives Matter protest that fans across the nation and around the world. A White House that has shut down—cut off—the coronavirus task force news briefings for more than a month. A June 1 military hit on peaceful protesters in Lexington Square—now Black Lives Matter Plaza. A solid 45 percent of American voters who believe implicitly everything the current president says and emulate everything he does.

Where are we? What does all of this chaos mean for us? Does the potential good justify the tragedy and near-tragedy that we are experiencing?

Donald Trump's "erratic stewardship" (a phrase I heard on the news) of the current crises is making many of us uneasy. Today he tweeted (in his own words) one of my favorite quotes—attributed to a number of historical figures: "Those that deny their history are doomed to repeat it!" He was responding to demands to rename some military bases. I wonder which of his historical advisers put those words in front of him? I doubt he's read enough to come up with any sort of historical reference.

A couple of days ago, I heard a description of Trump on MSNBC that, for me, seemed apt. He was described as "tone deaf" by Susan Page, *USA Today* Washington Bureau Chief.

Speaking of apt phrases, I was alarmed when I first saw the slogan "Defund the Police" painted on the street right next to "Black Lives Matter." "Defund the Police" has to do with the reallocation of police funds in the direction of social services, but it is defiantly negative and potentially threatening. I have subsequently heard much about this particular aspect of the protest, but my immediate response was that it was a mistake because it's open to misinterpretation, and that the Trump base would use it against the protesters. This quickly happened. In an interview, Nancy Pelosi said that she preferred "Justice in Policing"—not as catchy but infinitely better. There's no going back, of course. "Defund the Police" will be used against the protesters right up through the election.

Meanwhile, I'm still lonely. I'm essentially talking to myself. Hundreds of highly qualified politically astute analysts, columnists, reporters, and protesters are speaking for me. My hope is that this journal will be published at some point in the future and perhaps make a difference for those who read these words. It's what I hope for in my novels as well. I'm aiming for empathy—touching the reader with stories, essays, memoir—a sort of chronicle of a transforming year in all of our lives.

⌐⁓

On the first of June, when the protests were just starting, and some protesters were committing "crimes of opportunity," including looting, fires, and other types of destruction, I saw a news clip that has stayed with me, rather hauntingly. It took place in Los Angeles, in the Van Nuys area, with the police force clamping down on protesters all over the area. On the sidewalk, scattered over the now-deserted street, was the "loot" from a neighborhood drugstore: spilled bottles of prescriptions and prescription paperwork—that most personal of personal information—one's health data, one's medical records.

It struck me forcibly because, early in the days of our sheltering in place, a delivery of my prescriptions was stolen off my porch, without my knowledge. Even when the pills and paperwork were returned—in a plastic bag with the drugstore imprint—I did not immediately grasp the fact that my personal information, as well as the pills I put in my mouth every day, had been stolen, and then returned—apparently by some neighborhood thief who repented his theft, and tried to make amends when he saw that what he had stolen was useless except to the person from whom he had stolen. I felt violated, as though someone had invaded my home, my private space. The prescriptions were quickly replaced, but that sense of violation stayed with me, is with me still.

June 16, 2020

"Anyone care to guess who I am?" asked Charlie, from his quarter of the Zoom screen.

It was Sybil's idea to have the four book club friends join the next meeting wearing something "different" or "surprising," rather than their usual casual attire. They were to finish their discussion of Daniel Defoe's *A Journal of the*

Plague Year and move onto something more contemporary for their next read. She said it called for a celebration of sorts.

"Well," said Louise, pulling off her disposable face mask, "since you've put some sort of orange makeup on your face, and you have an orange Frisbee on your head, I can only guess you must be calling up our Commander in Chief—or—as Tony Schwartz calls him, our Psychopath in Chief."

"Who's Tony Schwartz?" asked Sybil. She was wearing dramatic eye makeup and an overload of costume jewelry.

Theresa, who had resurrected a flowered blue and yellow Easter Parade hat, a veil covering her eyes, spoke up.

"He ghostwrote *The Art of the Deal*, and he warned us about Trump way back in 2016."

"He's still warning us," said Louise. "That 'Psychopath in Chief' article was written last month. He quoted Trump as having said he had 'a very great relationship with God.'"

"Of course he does," said Charlie. "He's just behind the Pope in popularity with God."

"Speaking of God," said Sybil, "I'd like to thank Him for getting us to the end of this book—and any discussion that's left about it."

"I thought it was—timely," said Louise, who had suggested the book, "but, yes, it does go on and on—and on."

She waved the disposable mask in front of her.

"In case you're wondering, I was being my usual super-cautious self. I don't want to be the first person to catch the virus via a Zoom call."

"Anything's possible," said Sybil. "Does anyone have reading suggestions?"

"We need to pick something that helps us understand what the fuck's going on," Charlie chimed in, lifting the Frisbee off his head and tossing it across his "playroom." Fido could be heard in the background, barking in excitement as he chased it down.

"That's a big order," said Louise. "There's so *much* going on."

"I vote for *A Very Stable Genius*," said Charlie, rubbing at his orange makeup with a wad of tissues. "I know there's a lot of Trump stuff out there, but this was written by two *Washington Post* journalists. And—to speak to the general request—it's *very* contemporary."

"Well, we'd certainly be in the realm of the fake," said Sybil. "Our president has created a reality of his own. Any other suggestions?"

"I'll pass on making any suggestions for now," said Louise, "Defoe's work *did* seem appropriate."

"That leaves Theresa and me," said Sybil. "One of the Trump books might be an interesting pick. *The Room Where It Happened*, John Bolton's tell-all, will be out soon ..."

"Bolton had his chance during the impeachment process," said Charlie, angrily. "I'm not going to buy his fucking book."

Theresa carefully lifted her veil and removed her hat, fluffing her cropped salt and pepper hair.

"Does anybody remember that we're in the middle of a pandemic?" she asked. "Granted, it's sometimes hard to relate to a plague that happened in 1665, but shouldn't we stay on topic?"

"Why should we be different from the rest of the country?" said Charlie. "The pandemic has taken a back seat to George

Floyd, Rayshard Brooks, Black Lives Matter, gigantic protests, defunding the police, the upcoming election ..."

"It's hard to assess what's happening in real time," said Louise. "I guess that's why I suggested we go back in time."

Theresa persisted.

"How about *The Great Influenza*? It's certainly timely."

Sybil tugged impatiently at a chandelier earring. Louise and Charlie looked out impassively from their framed screens.

"It's about the 1918 pandemic," Theresa continued. "After *A Journal of the Plague Year*, we can relate to it, right?"

"I can't," said Sybil. She looked defiantly at the other Zoom faces.

Theresa huffed, audibly.

"Okay," said Sybil, relenting, "I'll settle for something more or less contemporary, and more or less topical—but not another plague epic."

Before anyone had a chance to respond, she spoke up again.

"Speaking of topical, did you see the family news conference last Saturday, the day after Rayshard Brooks was shot?"

"In the back—twice," Charlie added, suddenly irate. "By a cop who said, 'I got him' after he shot him down."

Sybil nodded. "He was only 27 years old, father of four. It was his daughter's eighth birthday."

"Here we go again," said Theresa. "Off topic."

"Sorry," said Sybil, lifting her chin, obviously not at all sorry, "but I found it so painful and yet—so moving."

"You're right, Sybil," said Louise. She often found herself mediating when the group discussion degenerated into argument. "We should focus on *all* the current issues in our reading."

There was a brief silence as the group pulled together the threads of their disjointed remarks, their faces thoughtful within their Zoom spaces.

Louise loved them all, despite their mild eccentricities. Charlie was outspoken, often blunt, with a wry sense of humor. Theresa was meticulous, conventional. Sybil was ardent in her views, searching for answers to pressing social and political issues. Louise herself, long since divorced and on her own, working freelance as a writer, had settled on philosophy to carry her through crisis and chaos.

"I suppose you've heard there's a movement to defund the Paw Patrol," said Charlie.

Sybil guffawed, her frame lighting up as she laughed.

"Trust Charlie to bring us back to reality," she said.

"I don't get it," said Theresa.

"It's a preschool TV show," said Louise, "but let's move on. Any last thoughts concerning *A Journal of the Plague Year*—my popular book club choice?"

"Like I said," Charlie responded. "It sucks."

"Can we give it a decent burial?" Louise responded. "I found myself identifying with so much that Defoe said as I read through the book. I thought it was eerily contemporary. I'll read a couple of passages from near the end."

Charlie groaned as Louise scanned her iPad and began to read.

... upon this notion spreading, viz., that the distemper was not so catching as formerly, and that if it was catched it was not so mortal, and seeing abundance of people who really fell

sick recover again daily, they took to such a precipitant cour-
age, and grew so entirely regardless of themselves and of the
infection, that they made no more of the plague than of an
ordinary fever, nor indeed so much.

"That does sound like us," commented Theresa.

"Except for the *viz*," quipped Charlie.

"It goes on to say that the physicians tried to stop them, printed warnings, and distributed them all over the city and suburbs, telling them that 'such a relapse might be more fatal and dangerous than the whole visitation had been already.' But nobody was listening."

She paused for a moment before she added, "He goes on, 'The consequence of this was ... above 3,000 fell sick that week ...'"

"The consequence of carelessness, ignorance, oblivious-ness" said Sybil. "A rush to normalcy, an inability to believe in something we can't see, feel, touch—until it kills us. That's what we're seeing now, for sure."

"That's exactly the point I wanted to make," said Louise.

"Well," said Charlie, "as you're our self-described super-cautious member, you'll note—the London plague *did* go away soon after, despite all that carelessness."

"It did decline, Charlie," said Louise, "after it killed a fifth of London's population—but it was still around the follow-ing year, when the Great Fire of London torched the city. So you might take a cue from our Psychopath in Chief. In case anything goes wrong, it helps to have a *great* relationship with God."

June 19, 2020

Late last night, catching up with the news on my iPhone, I saw a video clip of a masked California nurse, who said, "This is not a flu. This is a *monster.*"

She was referring to the spike in coronavirus cases in California. On June 17, the number of California cases per day surpassed 4,000. The exact number was 4,179. Daily cases in California have surpassed 2,000 since May 28. On March 13, the day I self-isolated, the number of cases was 45. A total of 5,362 California residents have died since then, 3,072 in LA County. What could possibly induce me to go out and about, even after fifteen weeks of isolation?

I sit at my desk every day looking out at the street from my two front windows. Despite Governor Newsom's mandatory order, issued yesterday, that everyone wear a mask in public, I don't see that order reflected on my quiet street. Whether taking a stroll, walking their dogs, or skateboarding, the mask-wearers are outnumbered by the bare-faced.

Mask-wearing has become a political statement, thanks to our president. He refuses to wear a mask in public, will not require those who attend tomorrow's indoor rally in Tulsa to wear a mask, and frequently makes fun of those who do—including Joe Biden. The pandemic, which has us by the throat, has become, in this country at least, a political pandemic—a monster that grows bigger and deadlier with each passing day.

There's no going back to normal, whatever that is, or was. Whether we're in phase 1 or phase 2 is immaterial. We're in a new world, a new reality. Everything looks just the same. The lovely cool "June gloom" California mornings are followed by sunshine and heat in the afternoon, then a cooling off again in the evenings. I treasure each day, knowing there will be unbearably hot days ahead. When those days come, I'll still be sheltering in place, chronicling events, trying to make sense of what I'm seeing, hearing, feeling—waiting for a release that is, in all likelihood, many months into the future.

⌒

Today, June 19, is Juneteenth. Juneteenth commemorates June 19, 1865, when Texas slaves were informed—two-and-a-half years after the event—that they had been freed. President Lincoln's Emancipation Proclamation was issued on January 1, 1863. On April 9, 1865, the Confederacy, under General Robert E. Lee, surrendered to General Ulysses S. Grant at Appomattox, Virginia. The Thirteenth Amendment was ratified on December 6, 1865—almost three years from beginning to end of that momentous turning point.

Juneteenth is very much in the news today because of Trump's upcoming rally in Tulsa, site of the 1921 "Black Wall Street" massacre in the Greenwood District of Tulsa. The massacre took place between May 31 and June 1—less than a mile from the convention center where tomorrow's rally will be held. I'm familiar with the Greenwood District massacre. The images from a documentary I saw long ago have lodged indelibly in my memory.

I grew up in a town that was quietly segregated. I didn't know at the time that it was segregated, nor did I think about it until I was an adult and had moved away. There were no obvious signs. There may have been a few black families living in the community. I didn't know them, however. I have had a number of social and business interactions with African Americans but no close black friends. I've been deprived, or have deprived myself, of adding another dimension to my experience. I feel that loss—especially today. What might I have done—what might I still do—to reach across that racial divide and make a more than nominal connection?

June 21, 2020

Yesterday's rally in Tulsa was a disaster—because poorly attended—for our egocentric president. He predicted huge crowds, set up an outside platform for the overload from the 19,000-capacity convention center. The outside venue was quietly dismantled when some 6,000 hardy, mostly bare-faced, cult followers turned up. Those who did turn up huddled close together inside, with vast rows of blue balcony seats totally empty. Trump's campaign officials claimed they received more than a million requests for tickets, that hundreds of thousands had been registered to attend. Local officials expected 100,000 to show up. Registrants were required to sign a waiver agreeing to "assume all risks" of coronavirus transmission as well as agreeing not to sue the campaign—but mask-wearing was optional.

It seems likely that a successful online prank (sign up but don't show up) is responsible for the under-attended rally, and Trump's humiliation.

⌣⌐

Statistics today, on May 21, and on April 21

Global cases:
9,031,796 (5,151,240) (2,500,156)
Global deaths:
469,526 (332,299) (171,810)

US cases:
2,354,275 (1,604,843) (800,932)
US deaths:
122,239 (95,656) (43,006)

California cases:
178,245 (84,057) (33,879)
California deaths:
5,518 (3,436) (1,225)

Los Angeles County cases:
83,397 (40,975) (13,816)
Los Angeles County deaths:
3,120 (1,976) (617)

June 26, 2020

Here we go again: back to the beginning. All the progress supposedly made since my self-incarceration on March 13 has been for naught. The country is back to square one. What a complete travesty. What a horrendous failure. Statistics today:

Global:
9,808,267 cases
  493,993 deaths

USA
2,527,025 cases
  127,055 deaths

California
201,004 cases
  5,809 deaths

LA County:
91,467 cases
  3,246 deaths

Daily new cases in California this week:

June 21	3,589
June 22	5,528
June 23	6,503
June 24	4,966
June 25	5,440
June 26	5,619

⌒

Where is the progress, in the most progressive state in the nation? Texas, Florida, and Arizona are also spiking—but that's not surprising, considering their total disregard for public health guidelines, and the fact that all three states have Republican governors. California, however—LA County, specifically—what's going on here? I'm mystified, but will continue looking for answers, wherever they may be hidden.

Today, VP Mike Pence, barefaced, mouthed the usual barefaced lies at the first coronavirus task force news briefing since April 27, saying that the country has made "truly remarkable progress in moving our nation forward" as we "open up America again."

Drs. Birx and Fauci stood on either side of him, wearing masks.

The briefing was kicked out of the White House and held, instead, at the Department of Health and Human Services.

June 28, 2020

No journal of the plague year 2020 (and most likely 2021) would be complete without paying homage to Instacart.

Food delivery services have become very popular during the pandemic. A lot of people, including me and my family, prefer to shop from home rather than risk getting infected by doing what we've been doing all of our lives—shopping at our local grocery stores.

As a young girl, I walked down the tranquil streets of my hometown to Main Street, the downtown area, where I shopped for my mother at Berk's Grocery Store. I ordered from the list my mother had given me, or just handed the list to the grocer. The clerk behind the counter—often Mr. Berk himself—did the shopping for me, interpreted my mother's written instructions, bagged the groceries, and handed the bags to me—a *fait accompli*.

Now, every two weeks or so, I sit down with my Instacart app and prepare a shopping list. It's like shopping online, only trickier, because someone else is about to shop for me in real time—someone I don't know, someone who doesn't know me. Most likely, that person has never shopped for me before and will never shop for me again. But he or she has elected to shop, for a fee and a tip, for those of us who elect to stay at home—and have a choice in the matter. That person—my shopper—is, of course, at risk for infection, as am I, if he or she doesn't take all of the precautions necessary. There's a strong element of trust—and distrust—in the transaction.

In pre-pandemic times, I did most of my shopping at three stores: Trader Joe's, Whole Foods, and Ralphs—with an occasional trip to Target. So far, I've chosen to shop at Ralphs (California's name for Kroger) because I can get most of what I need and want at a single store—whereas Trader Joe's is strictly for food (and isn't available via Instacart), and Whole Foods is for specialty food. Pre-pandemic, I shopped, on average, every week to ten days. Now I try to virtually shop no more than twice a month—which means I have to plan much more carefully than I ever have before.

I'm not a meal planner. I work with whatever's in the kitchen, make do with what I've got, or make a quick run to the store to buy cage-free eggs from Ralphs, pick up a fresh loaf of bread (still warm from the oven) at the Whole Foods bakery, or fill compostable plastic bags with organic apples, tomatoes, and Persian cucumbers at TJ's.

All that has changed—except for the time involved. I haven't done the math, but I'm quite certain that I spend as much time preparing my Instacart order, managing the Instacart shopping and delivery, wiping down the goods, cleaning up, as I did while shopping at my three or four chosen stores—including the driving.

Yesterday, working diligently, I prepared my Instacart grocery list. This morning, from about 8:30 to 9:30, I followed the shopper (Oliver) as he moved up and down the aisles at Ralphs, looking for the 27 items I had requested. I added instructions for each item: do not replace the antibacterial cleaner with regular cleaner (like last time); only salted organic butter to replace another salted organic butter; avoid gluten-free pasta at all costs. And so on.

While Oliver shopped, we exchanged several "chat" messages concerning items I had not listed: Are there any antiseptic wipes left in the world? (I didn't word it that way). Can you purchase more than one cube (65-count) box of facial tissues? (That's what I got last time.)

In addition, Oliver replaced several items, which I was asked to approve, and got a $1.99 refund (item unavailable). The items he successfully shopped were ticked off on my app, he checked out, and—lo and behold!—the grocery bags arrived at my door a slice of an hour later. I thanked him heartily (from inside the house) as he left.

I prep for the delivery as follows: I wash down the kitchen table and lay a long measuring stick down the center of the table. Then I bring the bags in from the porch, empty them bag by bag onto the left side of the table, wipe down each item with homemade wipes (paper towels dampened with spray cleaner and spritzed with antiseptic), and place the "clean" items on the right side of the table. I put freezer items away first, then refrigerated items, then the rest.

When I'm finally finished, it's a good feeling, and I wonder—why didn't I always do this? Why shouldn't I always wipe down the food and the packaging that I bring into my kitchen? But that's another story.

That's my Instacart routine. I'm getting used to it, and better at it. Out of six orders (two each in April, May, and June), two have been good experiences. The experience is getting better as I become a better Instacart shopper. Not surprising.

Right now, I can't see myself casually walking into a food market, rolling out a shopping cart, whisking an antiseptic wipe across the handlebar, then cruising up and down the aisles, making my way down my handwritten list, carefully checking ingredients and expiration dates, chatting with the cashier as I'm checked out. Those were the pre-pandemic years. Now it's back to Berk's Grocery Store—the proxy who does the shopping for me, who interprets my instructions, who makes decisions for me.

Whether Instacart is the contemporary version of Berk's—or Berk's was my childhood Instacart—I'm relying on the person in charge of my order to make good selections, to follow my instructions, to interpret my "chat" messages, to meet my expectations.

What's missing is the friendly feeling as I pulled open the door of that long-ago grocery store—to the tune of the little bell attached to the doorframe, announcing every arrival and exit.

June 29, 2020

California is spiking.

> Latest California stats:
> 222,444 cases/5,973 deaths

> Latest LA County stats:
> 100,772 cases/3,326 deaths

As far as the state of California and our very own LA County are concerned, it's gonna be a long, hot summer.

July 5, 2020

My family and I—and everyone else in LA County—are in the midst of a new and alarming pandemic surge. The numbers the last few days have kept climbing. As of today, LA County has 107,826 confirmed cases and 3,457 deaths. To put that in perspective, there have been 263,210 confirmed cases and 6,335 deaths in all of California.

U.S. cases are rising at a rate of more than 50,000 a day.

I feel suffocated by the numbers, by the confinement, by the relentless growth of this invisible "thing" that has immured me and everyone else who is paying attention.

My 4th of July was a non-event, except for a Zoom meeting with my writing group, FaceTime with family members, a few text-message exchanges with fireworks effects, and a couple of hours with a little dog (my Indi) *in extremis* while the sounds of fireworks exploded all around us.

On with the long, hot summer.

July 6, 2020

According to one analyst I heard today, as far as Covid-19 is concerned, we are in "free fall." California—LA County specifically—is front and center in terms of new cases. With a population somewhere between 14 million and 25 million (depending on how the area is counted), Los Angeles is the biggest and most populated county in the U.S.

⌒

California cases today:
277,433; +14,223 since yesterday.

LA County cases today:
116,570; +8,744 since yesterday.

July 13, 2020

My voluntary lockdown began in March, on Friday the 13th. Four months of incarceration.

I'm happy not to go out yet. I'm a willing hostage to the virus. I just wish the rest of the country would get in line with what's happening and do what's necessary: stay at home if possible; wear a mask; wash hands to the tune of "Row, Row, Row Your Boat" (as I wrote in a blog post); don't open up too soon!

Just heard on the news that LA schools will be online this fall. Thank God, our governor, mayor, and school superintendent are intelligent, caring adults—not puppets following the directive of a subhuman president. There is no good answer to reopening schools in the next few weeks. We are, as a nation—and in LA—in crisis mode. We can't experiment with our children. This out-of-control pandemic has inflicted enough panic, pandemonium, and death, without putting every child and every teacher—as well as their families—at risk.

July 14, 2020

"I still say *A Very Stable Genius* would have been a good pick," said Charlie, when they met again on Zoom, "but I'm okay with Toni Morrison."

"You're 'okay' with a Nobel-Prize-winning novelist?"

Theresa's voice was acidic.

"Sorry, Charlie," said Sybil. "I hear there have been more than sixty books written about Donald Trump since he became president. Don't we get enough of him in the news?"

"Obviously not," Charlie replied. "He's our national bad boy. We get off reading about the murky depth of his badness."

Sybil spoke up.

"I think *The Bluest Eye* is a good choice. It was published fifty years ago but, like all important fiction, it's still relevant."

"It is, in part, about violence," said Louise, thoughtfully. "Violence against poor blacks; violence against poor black women; violence within poor black families, including the family of Pecola Breedlove."

"I haven't gotten through the book," said Charlie, "but right up front, in the prologue, we learn Pecola has been raped by her father and had a baby who died. No suspense there. We know what happens before the story begins."

Sybil spoke up.

"I'd like to discuss that prologue. Here's how it begins."

She propped the book in front of her and began to read.

Quiet as it's kept, there were no marigolds in the fall of 1941. We thought, at the time, that it was because Pecola was having her father's baby that the marigolds did not grow.

Sybil raised her eyes momentarily, glancing at the faces of her friends, then went on.

What is clear now is that of all of that hope, fear, lust, love, and grief, nothing remains but Pecola and the unyielding earth. Cholly Breedlove is dead, our innocence too. The seeds shriveled and died; her baby too.

"So," said Theresa, "Morrison is telling us that the story is about the loss of innocence—for Claudia, the narrator, and her sister, as well as for Pecola."

"Can we even have this discussion?" said Charlie, stroking his gray-streaked stubble.

"I understand what you're saying, Charlie," said Louise. "We haven't had that experience. But isn't that Toni Morrison's gift? We have to *start* somewhere."

"I agree," said Sybil. "I have black friends, but most of them are successful. They look and act like me. We need to dig down deep into the soul of the black experience—and it has been, for many, a tragic experience."

"There's a pervading element of violence in this book," Louise went on, "as there is in the black experience—as there is for all of us right now. Maybe it's just me, but I feel it more, now, in my self-imposed isolation."

Louise paused, rubbed her forehead, as if to force her thoughts into a logical sequence.

"Incest is, perhaps, the ultimate act of violence toward one's own—and Cholly is guilty of that—but there are so many levels of violence—toward one's own people but also toward anyone—*anyone*—who challenges our norms."

No one spoke. They were waiting for Louise to continue.

"Earlier this month, in southern France, a bus driver was beaten to death because he asked several of his passengers to put on masks. It was a requirement for transportation on the bus. The driver was pushed off the bus and beaten savagely around the head by two of the passengers. He died a few days later, after being diagnosed as brain dead."

Louise checked the faces on her computer screen, but no one spoke up.

"A few days later, a Michigan man at a convenience store stabbed a 77-year-old customer for asking him to cover his face. The man, who refused to cover his face and instead stabbed the customer, was later shot by police for threatening them with the knife. He died in surgery.

"I'm sure there are many more stories like these. There's so much *hostility* in the air. Where will it end? *When* will it end? Pecola's story touches me because there is so much *yearning* in her. If she could only drink enough white milk out of a Shirley Temple cup, maybe she would *become* white. Maybe her eyes would turn blue. If she could look out at the world with blue eyes, maybe the ugliness she saw around her—the ugliness she thought she saw every time she looked in the mirror—would disappear."

"I like the Shirley Temple cup episode," said Sybil. "She's staying with Claudia and her sister, Frieda, for a few days, and she's so enamored with this little movie star girl, with her blue eyes, her curls, her whiteness, that she drinks three quarts of milk out of a blue-and-white Shirley Temple cup. She literally *drinks* the whiteness she craves!"

"For Pecola," Louise summed up, "the essence of beauty is having blue eyes."

"So what makes it so relevant?" said Charlie. "I'm relieved we've moved from 1665 to the 20th century, but we're still in the past. The story takes place in the early 1940s, in Lorain, Ohio—"

"Where Morrison herself grew up," Theresa interjected. Louise nodded.

"It's obvious, Charlie, from the beginning of this story, that black lives didn't much matter back then. Even more, black *girls'* lives didn't matter. We're learning every day, from racist rhetoric that trickles from the top down, that not much has changed since then."

Theresa spoke up again.

"The young girl, Pecola, is obsessed with beauty—specifically, white beauty. She comes to stay with Claudia and her family for a few days after Pecola's father"—she glanced down at her book—"'that old Dog Breedlove had burned up his house, gone upside his wife's head, and everybody, as a result, was outdoors.'"

"I've been thinking a lot about this book," said Louise, before Sybil had a chance to respond, "as I go through my lockdown days, reading, watching the news, trying to assess the pandemic, worrying about the upcoming election, wondering why my house isn't cleaner when I'm at home so much ..."

Her voice drifted off.

"I don't know how to process ..."

Feeling a landslide of emotions threatening to engulf her, Louise cleared her throat and continued.

"I can't really comprehend the death and disruption, the hostility and anger, that are everywhere around us right now ...

"We're privileged. We're shielded from the worst of it to some degree. But it's out there. People are dying by the hundreds of thousands. The threat of death permeates everything—everything we touch, every breath we take. And people are *killing* each other over the polemics of wearing a face covering. Somehow—not just in this country—there are people who have come to equate the wearing of a mask with mindless conformity, the absence of a mask with freedom.

"Like any important work, *The Bluest Eye* is not just about the black experience. It's about the *human* experience, and how we respond to life—and death. Pecola Breedlove is a victim of abuse and violence—but she survives. She descends into madness—but she survives. I wonder—is the choice to survive the real and ultimate test? Not the quality of one's life, but life itself?"

July 14, 2020

A *New York Times* headline just caught my attention—in a most alarming way. Apparently, the Trump administration has ordered hospitals to "bypass" the Centers for Disease Control and Prevention (CDC) and, instead, send all Covid patient information to a central database in Washington, DC.

Dr. Birx, it seems, complained that hospitals were not adequately reporting their data and subsequently she and her officials devised a "new" plan with, potentially, political motivation.

We may not get accurate data on the virus from tomorrow forward. I am now concerned that Dr. Birx has put herself in the president's pocket.

The word "alarming" cannot be repeated too often.

July 17, 2020

Congressional Representative and Civil Rights leader John R. Lewis died today. He was 80 years old. His 1965 beating by state troopers in Selma, Alabama, during a voting rights demonstration, led to passage of the 1965 Voting Rights Bill.

⟜⟝

Next week, Joe Biden will announce his choice for vice president. We know it will be a woman. If it's a black woman, I believe there will be no turning back. If not—we may not get the votes needed to win the election. The black vote is critical to this election.

Fortunately, there are a number of black women who are well qualified for the position. He has—to use that somewhat comical word—a "plethora" of candidates from which to choose. CNN (among other news outlets) reports that among the black women being considered are Sen. Kamala Harris of California, Rep. Val Demings of Florida, Atlanta Mayor Keisha Lance Bottoms, former Obama administration National Security Adviser Susan Rice, and Rep. Karen Bass of California.

My first choice has always been Kamala Harris—perhaps because I know her best, from the debates. I like her feistiness. She'll be problematic if she's selected. She came down hard on Biden during the debates; she has to defend decisions made in her prosecutorial background; she's not "easy." But that's a good contrast for Joe Biden, who is reassuringly easygoing and transparent.

The other big question mark in the upcoming election is the voting process itself. Will there be time to put a lid on the innumerable voter suppression tactics throughout the country? Will the John R. Lewis Voting Rights Act 2020 be passed by the Senate in time to make a difference?

"There will be no turning back," Lewis said of the recent

Black Lives Matter movement, which he called "massive" and "all inclusive."

There will be no turning back if we win this election. Our country, crippled and wounded as it is, will heal.

There will be no turning back if we lose this election. Our country will dissolve into an unrecognizable autocratic police state.

July 20, 2020

Portland, Oregon, is the president's preview of the police state he is attempting to establish. Today, on Fox TV, he said he would like to send his unmarked secret police force to all of our major cities—New York, Chicago, Oakland, Philadelphia, Baltimore—he stopped there; other cities were implied. Trump called the protesters in these cities "anarchists."

In Portland, faceless, helmeted, unmarked troops, acting without a warrant, without identification, are rounding up peaceful protesters, escorting them to unmarked cars (I've heard the cars are from local rentals), and driving off. There is no interaction, no charge, no identification, no response to onlookers repeatedly demanding names, insignia, charges, from these nameless federal agents.

This is our autocratic president's idyllic state: an environment in which there is no protest because protesters disappear into the maw of his making. Perhaps they'll reappear; perhaps not.

I am frightened by the possibilities of what this deranged man might accomplish in the upcoming three months—and how he might undercut our single most powerful weapon of counterattack: the November 3 vote.

I intend to vote by mail soon after I get the ballot in the mail, so there's no possibility my vote will be delayed at the Post Office. I'm not going to concern myself with the various "measures" that usually delay my response as I try (with varying degrees of success) to understand the pros and cons. My vote—down-the-line Democratic—will be in the mail *post haste.*

⌒

The first case of Covid-19 in the United States was recorded on January 20, 2020, in Snohomish County, north of Seattle. The patient was a 35-year-old man who had returned home after visiting family members in Wuhan, China.

Six months ago today.

The U.S. is now documenting more than 25 percent of coronavirus cases worldwide.

The U.S. population is 4 percent of the world population.

Current World Stats
Total cases: 14,845,960
Total deaths: 612,841
One-day increase in cases: 205,624

Current U.S. Stats
Total cases: 3,961,429
Total deaths: 143,834
One-day increase in cases: 62,879

July 23, 2020

It's about 2:45 p.m. I'm watching the White House coronavirus briefing on my iPhone as I go through my email.

At the start of the (solo) briefing (Dr. Birx was in the room but did not speak), when I heard Trump say the words, "China virus," I had an intense physical reaction. It was so heart-stopping I had to halt what I was doing; I had to collect my thoughts; I had to collect my physical being.

After talking about why we must keep schools open, bragging about the stock market, and announcing the cancellation of the "live" RNC, he said:

"I spoke to President Putin today."

I had to stop again, collect myself again, put myself together again.

Then, in discussing the shutdown of our country, he said:

"We had to turn it off because of what China did."

After a half hour, which included accepting a few questions from respectful reporters, he left the podium, and that was that: our coronavirus update.

I'm still feeling ill.

July 29, 2020

On MSNBC this afternoon, Congressman Jim Clyburn (D-SC) referred to the Republican Party as "sinister."

Interesting word choice. Kinda perfect. Fits in well with the latest Trump pushback, in which he says that reports of Russian bounties on U.S. troops are "fake news."

⌒

Also ...

It's official. We've surpassed the 150,000-count in death-by-coronavirus.

Current U.S. Stats
Total cases: 4,560,336
Total deaths: 153,583
One-day increase in cases: 61,784

Or maybe it's *not* official. I used worldometer.com for my stats. I did a little research on Covid-19 stats yesterday. There is, apparently, a great deal of variance in the methods used and results emanating from statistical sites.

Here, for instance, are the CDC stats for today:

Total cases: 4,339,997
Total deaths: 148,866
One-day increase in cases: 59,862

I also looked up (slightly different) stats from Johns Hopkins University and *The New York Times*. I'm sure there are many other sources I could access, but these stats are depressing enough for me.

July 30, 2020

Trump tweeted, at 5:46 a.m. EDT, that the 2020 election will be the most inaccurate and fraudulent election in history.

Except that he tweeted, "the most INACCURATE & FRAUDULENT Election in history."

Why settle for standard English composition when the all-caps key is handy?

His fix: "Delay the Election."

〜

Barack Obama, at today's funeral of John R. Lewis at Ebenezer Baptist Church, Atlanta, called for "expanded ballot access." He suggested that we honor Lewis's legacy by expanding the Voting Rights Act.

Obama said that, even though "we no longer have to guess the number of jellybeans in a jar in order to cast a ballot" (an accurate historical reference), there are "those in power" who are attacking our voting rights "with surgical precision."

〜

Donald Trump at Covid-19 news brief, 6:00 p.m. EDT:

[re people getting sick]
"It's China's fault."
[and again]
"It's China's fault."

⌢

Haiku

Jellybeans in a
jar guess how many there are
if you want to vote.

It's China's fault it's
China's fault it's China's fault
it's China's fault it's

Ninety-six days to
endure the current regime.
We shall overcome.

July 31, 2020

"Three Men and a Baby"

The 1987 movie was referenced by *The New York Daily News* in their reporting on the John Lewis funeral in Atlanta yesterday. Three former presidents—Barack Obama, George W. Bush, and Bill Clinton—honored Lewis with their presence and their words, while the current president ignored the event, choosing instead to tweet that the upcoming election, if we vote by mail, will be "inaccurate," "fraudulent," and perhaps should be delayed until everyone can vote in person.

I'm hearing the word "fascism" more and more as I read, listen to, and watch news and news commentary. Today, on MSNBC, Tom Nichols, senior advisor for The Lincoln Project, said we're not there yet, but we may be on our way to fascism. He also said to turn our attention from Trump, who's fizzling out, to Bill Barr, who's the real power behind the throne. He described the others in the president's inner circle as "clowns."

The Lincoln Project ads—especially "Mourning in America"—are excellent.

August 2, 2020

Today, SpaceX returned safely to earth with NASA astronauts Bob Behnken and Doug Hurley. It was the first astronaut trip into orbit by a private company, a "historic" 64-day flight, and the first water landing (in the Gulf of Mexico) by NASA astronauts since 1975.

In true Trump headline-grabbing fashion, one of the pleasure boats that surrounded the recovery team shortly after touchdown displayed a large "Trump for President" flag.

August 5, 2020

Three months to go till Election Day—although that particular day seems to be increasingly irrelevant. There's early voting. There's mail-in voting. There are post-election-day voting tallies. There's a president trying his damndest to undermine the voting process. There's Russia doing everything it can to get its puppet president back in the driver's seat.

I can't think. I can't write. I'm tired. I'm lethargic. I can't seem to move forward with anything. It's almost 6:30 p.m. I'm ready to quit, and not just for the evening. The only thing that will get me going again is (1) a surprising monetary windfall or (2) an inspirational bout of writing.

What am I doing? Does it have any value? I'm attempting to harness this singular moment in history, from both a personal and factually documented perspective—often both at the same time. And I'm trying—hopefully, with some success—to write a fictional account of this time in our collective lives. I want to understand, to convey, what is going on in the world and in the country of my birth. Right now.

Nothing is as it should be. Everything is distorted by the pandemic, and by the corruption within the government in its packaging of the pandemic. Disorder within disease within global chaos. I can't stomach it. I want to vomit.

We'll reach 160,000 dead and five million cases in the United States very soon. Meantime, some innocent children in this country are going back to school—not, thank God, in LA.

I looked this up earlier this afternoon (source: National Center for Education Statistics). In the state of California, the student/staff ratio, including teaching, administrative, and all other support staff, is about 60/40. The ratio in other states varies, but 30 to 40 percent support staff seems to be the average. That means, in California, if students had been ordered to go back to school, as they have been in some states, more than six million children and 2.5 million support staff would have been at risk. This seems to be what Trump and his enablers want. Although he talks about the pandemic in his daily news briefs, Twitter feeds, and interviews, the potential human carnage does not seem to penetrate whatever brain matter lies beneath that orange Frisbee on his head.

No conscience. No empathy. No soul.

August 11, 2020

Tuesday afternoon, 1:20 p.m.: California's Senator Kamala Harris has just been announced as the VP pick.

Joe Biden could not have done better. He chose the woman who challenged him unmercifully at the presidential nomination debates—and he rose above it. She will be the bulldog at his side—both loyal and fearless. She complements him. She is his antithesis in many ways, and that is what makes them a formidable team. In addition, they represent two distinct generations. She was a friend of Biden's late son, Beau, who was a few years younger than Kamala.

It's twelve weeks before Election Day. Now we have a chance—and our chances are good. I was worried that former National Security Advisor Susan Rice would be the pick—and the Biden team would be labeled "Old School" and have to deal with past baggage. Or that Sen. Elizabeth Warren would be chosen and the Biden team labeled "Socialist," a Bernie Sanders lookalike team—not to mention the blowback from black female voters. Or that a candidate would be chosen because she could shore up a red state—Florida's Rep. Val Demings, Michigan's Gov. Gretchen Whitmer, Atlanta's Mayor Keisha Lance Bottoms, or former Georgia State Rep. Stacey Abrams—all of whom are qualified but not my first pick.

The obvious advantage for all of the women considered is that they have been put in the national spotlight and will have a noticeable advantage as they move forward with their careers. I believe this might have been part of Joe Biden's strategy as he created and extended the suspense around the candidates. He was career-boosting as well as considering potential VPs.

Kamala Harris, in my opinion, is the strongest and most experienced of the candidates. She is the best choice. Trump has already responded, calling her "nasty," one of his favorite descriptors for women he finds challenging.

August 13, 2020

Charlie, Sybil, and Theresa were greeting each other from their now-familiar Zoom rectangles. Louise peeked with friendly interest at the backdrop of each frame—Charlie's studio, which he called his "playroom"; Sybil's pristine and well-equipped kitchen; Theresa's traditionally furnished living room, her two regal cats licking their paws on the French provincial sofa.

Louise sat in her book-lined study, elbow on her desk, chin resting on the back of her hand, eyes glancing from one rectangle to another. Although she looked forward to meeting with her friends online, she missed the pre-pandemic days, when they met in each other's homes, when they shared the same space, the same food and drink, when they weren't stacked like Lego building blocks on a computer screen.

"Do you remember *The West Wing*?" Charlie asked, when the chatter died down.

Louise spoke up.

"You mean that show about the old days, when our president and his staff were motivated by intelligence and high moral standards?"

"Yeah, that's the one," Charlie replied. "So, I was watching—okay, re-watching—an early episode the other night. Josh, the deputy chief of staff, says, in effect, that we don't need to worry about nuclear attacks. All we need is an epidemic, like an outbreak of smallpox, and we can wipe out a big chunk of humanity."

"Aaron Sorkin was right, but he wasn't the first," Sybil responded. "It was common knowledge in the scientific community. We were warned. Over and over. By virologists. By experts. I read books on viruses *years* ago. We've had plagues all through history. We've had multiple global pandemics in the past two hundred years—in the 1840s and 50s, as well as in 1918—the one Trump persists in calling the '1917' pandemic."

Louise pressed the mute button. The rectangles lit up one by one as the discussion went on, but she didn't want to hear it. Her casement windows opened onto a small terrace, the tip of a waterfall gushing from the fountain in its center. When she muted her screen, she could hear its soothing whisper.

She thought about what her doctor had said to her yesterday. *"Take it easy. Don't fret. You can't change everything that's wrong with the world. You have to look after your own health. The stress is taking a toll on your heart."*

My heart, she thought—100,000 beats a day; nine million times in the last three months. Hard work, even in the best of health. I wonder if it will take me through this time-out-of-time. I wonder if I'll survive. If I get the virus, I might die. If I don't get the virus, the stress could kill me. Where am I in my life? Somewhere in the final movement? The allegro vivace is long past—that energetic scherzo period played itself out somewhere between the millennium and the pandemic. This might be the finale—hopefully a graceful, dignified coda.

Meantime, I'm pretty much going it alone. No kids, like Charlie and Theresa. No full-time job. My working days— commute and cubicle—are probably behind me. Relatives? A former husband doesn't count, so it's just my sister and her kids. I have friends scattered all over the country, but right now those three rectangles on my Zoom screen contain my closest friends.

She unmuted her screen.

"Can we talk about *The Bluest Eye* now?"

Always hypersensitive to everyone's mood, she felt rather than heard the rising tension as the Zoom frames lit up again and again.

She was aware that, like herself, her friends found solace in the time they spent together, despite their differences—or perhaps because of them, because their time together was a diversion from the numbing persistence of the pandemic— and from more personal matters. She knew—from private conversations—that Charlie and Joan had discussed a separation, that Sybil was sometimes desperately lonely in her still-transitional role as a doctor's second wife, that Theresa felt increasingly isolated as she coped with the death of her husband, Turk, and the absence of her grown children.

There was a perilous side-effect to the pandemic, Louise thought, as the other frames stilled—what Michelle Obama had described a few days ago as "low-grade depression." She was feeling it, and she had little doubt her friends were feeling it as well.

"The story is simple," she began. "Pecola Breedlove, eleven years old, is growing up in Lorain, Ohio, in 1940. She is poor. She considers herself ugly. She has one wish: to have blue eyes. Blue eyes, she has convinced herself, will bring her beauty, happiness, admiration.

"After she is raped by her drunken father, after she bears a child, who dies, she descends into madness. But she has triumphed, in a way, because, in her madness, she believes she is in possession of the one attribute that will shield her from a world that has ignored and, ultimately, disowned her."

She found her place in the book and read from it.

A little black girl yearns for the blue eyes of a little white girl, and the horror at the heart of her yearning is exceeded only by the evil of fulfillment.

Sybil spoke up.

"There *is* a success story that we can now paste side-by-side with Pecola's sad story, and that's the story of Kamala Harris."

"Harris is more Claudia than Pecola" said Louise. "Claudia is Toni Morrison looking back on her childhood. She's poor and black but she has caring parents. Pecola has no one and nothing but this 'yearning.'"

"Then how is it relevant?" asked Sybil. "Why are we reading it?"

Louise spoke up again.

"Because 'the bluest eye' is a metaphor for everything the African American community yearns for and aspires to—recognition, acceptance, equality. Kamala Harris is the embodiment of that metaphor."

"We could have done better," said Theresa, sounding more peevish than usual. "I make no apologies for backing Bernie Sanders and Elizabeth Warren."

"None asked for," said Charlie. "I think Kamala Harris is a great VP pick. She's a fighter, and she's fearless, although—like Theresa says—she's not universally liked by Dems. But what about political reality? We put Barack Obama in the White House for eight years, but we still went on to elect a racist and a hatemonger. Who's to say we've learned anything? Who's to say we won't do it again?"

"It's like the pandemic," said Sybil. "We think we've stamped out bigotry in so many areas of our lives, and then it comes back—or erupts in another area."

Louise spoke up.

"For Pecola, back in the 1940s, there was no lesson learned, and no way out. She was literally stripped of her selfhood. Claudia and her family were kind to Pecola, but it was already too late. Her fixation became the dominant impulse of her life—her justification for abandoning reality. I would imagine ..."

She stopped to think, then continued.

"I would guess we all have our fixations—something that we keep close—secret—but something that, however imaginary—however much based on hope rather than on reality—makes us feel good about ourselves, makes our lives bearable."

"It's like living up to someone you don't know, you only know *about*," said Sybil. "You do your damnedest, but you wonder if you'll ever quite make the grade."

The faces in the rectangles were pensive, knowing Sybil was thinking about her husband Greg's first wife. Then Charlie spoke up.

"Are we delusional—not like Pecola but in our own way, in our own time? The country is about evenly divided between Biden and Trump. Historically, most of our presidents have been reelected for a second term. Who's to say it won't happen again in November? There's a solid base that believes Trump has the bluest eyes. It doesn't seem to matter what he says or does. He's responsible for the death of tens of thousands of Americans who need not have died. He's openly dismantling the Post Office so the mail-in ballot will be crippled. He's defied our norms for four years. And let's not forget he was impeached! But odds are still 50/50 he'll be reelected. We ignore that at our peril."

They looked at one another, silently acknowledging the threat Charlie described.

Sybil was the first to respond. She and Charlie had a special connection that Louise recognized, although she only suspected its basis.

"Charlie, I wish I could sit beside you and hold your hand. I'd tell you not to worry. I'm here for you. We're here for you. We'll get through this, together. And even if I go away, like Pecola's friend, for a little while, I'll be back. That's a promise."

Charlie gave her a one-handed high five but did not respond.

After a pause, Louise spoke up.

"Real or imaginary, we need friends in our lives, especially now. We need one or two or three people who accept us and believe in us, and we need ..."

She hesitated; then Sybil's frame lit up.

"The 'thing with feathers,'" said Sybil.

Louise nodded vigorously.

"For now," said Louise, "and especially for the next few months, I need all of you and—in Emily Dickinson's words—'the thing with feathers.'"

August 17, 2020

The virtual Democratic Convention starts today at 7:00 p.m. The polls are getting closer. Trump still has his finger on the economy, and the allegiance of voters who believe the economy is primary. For many, it seems, the economy is what matters. The pandemic is secondary. Crippling the Post Office prior to mail-in voting—the latest autocratic move—is secondary. Dismantling sorting equipment and removing our universal blue drop-off boxes is secondary. The president of our country is corrupt, a would-be autocrat. He'd like to be a president with no term limits. He cannot open his mouth without lying. It is a sad, depressing, and demoralizing time.

Robert Trump, the president's youngest brother, died over the weekend. He was 71. Trump visited him at a New York City hospital on Friday. His brother died on Saturday.

So far, no cause of death has been disclosed. According to an article I read, even Robert Trump found it impossible to work for Donald Trump. In the 1980s, Donald Trump put his brother in charge of an Atlantic City casino project. After a catastrophic opening weekend, a furious Donald Trump denounced his younger brother. Robert Trump walked out on him and never worked for his brother again.

My father didn't give out a lot of advice, but I remember his saying, more than once, "Never work with your relatives."

August 18, 2020

The 19th Amendment:

> *"The right of citizens of the United States to vote shall not be denied or abridged by the United States or by any State on account of sex. Congress shall have power to enforce this article by appropriate legislation."*

Today marks the 100th anniversary of the 19th Amendment. It's a good date to remember, and yet—it's not the only date to remember, as I've read in recent news stories.

An opinion piece in *The New York Times* reminds us that many additional steps were required to give voting rights to *all* women—that the process took another half-century—and that the voting rights of African American women were continually challenged during that time.

August 20, 2020

In many respects, the Democratic National Convention is a yawn. The effort to make a virtual event somehow lively often falls flat. There are a few exceptions, however. The state-by-state roll call was a winner. Seeing the delegates in their native states, in their geographic surroundings, was wonderful. I watched it with awe. What a country we live in! Not just superhighways taking us from one place to another but the reality of provincial accents, the beauty of natural surroundings, the diversity of citizens and cultures. I doubt we'll ever go back to delegates in a crowded space wearing funny hats and screaming out their state's unique qualities.

Other than that, there were the speeches. Michelle Obama. Barack Obama. Hilary Clinton. Kamala Harris. I hope those on the fence were watching and listening. This is our last chance. If Trump is re-elected—and the latest polls say he might be—our democracy is dead. We will become an autocracy, with little control over the autocrat-in-charge. Our environment will be decimated. Our rights, including our voting rights, will be critically impacted. The legal system will crumble. Our place in world politics will continue its rapid descent. Immigration obstruction will resume its disastrous course.

And, of course, there's the immediate effect on our health and our lives, as the Covid-19 virus decimates our country. Lives will continue to be lost that could have been saved. The virus will continue its erratic course, while a totally inept administration shifts both responsibility and blame onto the states.

I'm terrified that much of this might come to be, and that not enough people are listening to the message the Democrats are sending out via the Democratic National Convention, and the virtual campaign. Trump will put himself and his cult out there, in smaller crowds than he wants, but nevertheless in live events. He doesn't care about lives lost. He sees no value in setting an example of distancing and mask-wearing. He wants to win. That's what makes him tick. If he loses, he'll be inundated with lawsuits. If he loses, his access to a national microphone, on a daily and hourly basis, will go away. If he loses, he will be in the unthinkable position of—a loser.

Tonight is the fourth and final night of the DNC. Joe Biden will speak. He is, in my opinion, one of the good guys. Hopefully, he'll give a memorable speech. But, even if he does give a moving, hopeful, decisive speech, will he move the undecided voter who is still straddling that virtual fence? Will he continue to be strong in the swing states, right through October? Will the votes be counted accurately? Will the Post Office survive this month's attack? Mail-sorting equipment ripped out of post offices all over the country. Blue mailboxes removed from their concrete foundations, loaded onto trucks, and removed to—who knows where, with who knows what mail still locked inside those steel tummies?

And, if Trump loses, will he walk out of the White House and out of our national nightmare? Or will he call the election a "fraud" and a "hoax," discount the results, refuse to leave? Will the nightmare scenario be prolonged as we are plunged into yet another dark dream corridor—while the frightening spectacle of the last four years continues?

August 27, 2020

I'm not watching the Republican Convention. I've tuned in for a few minutes here and there this week, but the language, the lies, the unreality of it upsets me so much that I'm compelled to turn it off. The dismissal of all previous campaign norms is stunning—including speaking from the White House and the Rose Garden (after decimating the latter), and a political speech from Secretary of State Mike Pompeo while on duty in Jerusalem. All of these activities violate the Hatch Act, a 1939 law that limits the commingling of political activity and government business. I was not familiar with the Hatch Act—apparently because it has never before been so blatantly ignored.

The pandemic, not surprisingly, is either ignored or presented as under control, with the country well on its way to a speedy recovery. There are, apparently, no limits to the lengths this administration will go to distort reality.

Tonight is the final night of the RNC "Unreality Show" (my appellation). Trump will speak from the White House, again using the backdrop to sanction his lies. With 1,500 people assembled on the White House lawn, he will have the live audience that feeds his insatiable ego, and hear the sound he craves more than any other—the sound of applause. Masks are recommended but not mandatory. Truth is recommended but not anticipated.

Since August 15, more than one million acres have gone up in flames in Northern California. In Louisiana, last night, there was "an extremely dangerous Category 4 hurricane," with "catastrophic storm surge, extreme winds and flash flooding." Thousands of people displaced and dumped into a world contaminated with Covid-19. What could be worse than losing one's home amid flames or 150-mph winds—in the midst of an uncontrolled pandemic? What's happening to those unfortunate people caught in a double-bind catastrophe? In a crisis, social distancing and other standard precautions are challenging—maybe impossible. More Covid cases. Potentially, more lives lost.

Plague. Fire. Flood. Hurricane. Death and destruction everywhere. It's like the end of the world. And yet—at the other end of the spectrum—people like me, quietly waiting out the pandemic, hoping not to be challenged by natural disaster, grateful for our continuing health, and the health and safety of our families and friends.

Meantime, the protests go on, as police continue to kill or critically injure unarmed black men without adequate cause: George Floyd, May 25, Minneapolis; Rayshard Brooks, June 12, Atlanta. The latest: Jacob Blake, August 23, Kenosha, Wisconsin—in critical care after being shot in the back seven times as he tried to get into his car.

"Black men are an endangered species," according to a professional athlete, one of many protesting the Jacob Blake shooting by boycotting their own pro teams.

August 31, 2020

"Hope" is the thing with feathers

"Hope" is the thing with feathers –
That perches in the soul –
And sings the tune without the words –
And never stops – at all –

And sweetest – in the Gale – is heard –
And sore must be the storm –
That could abash the little Bird
That kept so many warm –

I've heard it in the chillest land –
And on the strangest Sea –
Yet – never – in Extremity,
It asked a crumb – of me.

—Emily Dickinson

I need the warmth of this poem right now. I feel—in so many ways—hopeless. The election is only weeks away, and Trump continues to do things that make me abandon all hope. The latest: denying Congress in-person access to intelligence reports—including election threats.

And, of course, there are the numbers: six million coronavirus cases confirmed in the U.S.; 25 million cases worldwide—and the polls, which show Trump neck-and-neck with Biden.

September 2, 2020

The solution seems so simple, and yet—so out of reach. Warning signs have been showing up everywhere, for years, for decades.

Here's how I see it: We have steadily destroyed and/or reduced the natural habitats for many species—including such known disease carriers as bats and rats. Those creatures, and many others, have been forced to live in areas increasingly closer to the invading species—we humans, as well as our domesticated animals. This propinquity, and the resulting interaction with species for which we have no natural immunity, have resulted in the spread of viruses—currently, "Coronavirus Disease 2019," or Covid-19.

Each incident of extreme weather—wildfires, floods, record-breaking high temperatures and high winds, hurricanes, melting glaciers—underscores our failure to put the brakes on the wholesale destruction of our environment.

Our current president's ignorance of and disdain for science, data, expertise, environmental concerns, have blunted and redirected our response to the seemingly obvious solution to both the pandemic and extreme weather conditions—environmental responsibility. Instead of focusing on this goal, we've been forced to turn our attention to the short-term tactics needed to survive and control our immediate crises. Who knows how many lives have been lost because of Trump's ineptitude in dealing strategically with the pandemic? The damage to our environment preceded him and continues with him.

We cannot bring back those lost lives, but the environmental damage is not irreparable if, two months from now, we elect a president who sees the big picture and can move forward with strength and integrity. Joe Biden has, roughly, a fifty-fifty chance. I'm hopeful, but not sanguine, about the outcome.

September 10, 2020

I love September—the clarity of it, the brilliant sunlight, the warmth—sometimes intense—ameliorated by gently moving air. September is a month of blue skies, cool nights, the whisper of dry leaves.

The sky today is a somber, uniform gray, a constant reminder of the more than three million acres burning in California—with more fires in neighboring states. In Australia, more than 25 million acres have burned in recent months. Are we on the same path—not tens of thousands of acres burned (as in previous years) but millions of acres? Our world, it seems, is on fire.

I feel like the sky—gray, gloomy. Everything is eerie, unreal. It's as though I were in a dream. But I'm not. I'm safe in my home, looking out at an unfamiliar world.

There are so many people in my adopted state who lost their homes—and some who lost their lives. Beyond the loss of human life, I feel so acutely the pain of the wildlife that has been snuffed out in the midst of this fiery devastation. Unlike human life and death, we'll never be able to accurately count the wildlife, or to know their pain, their terror, as they tried to escape. I hope the smoke rendered many of them mercifully unconscious before the flames moved in. And the trees; the creatures that fly, that nest, in those trees; those that creep and crawl on the earth; the insects upon which they feed; the unseen, perhaps undocumented plant life. So much life gone, perhaps never to return because of the double stress of fire and near-extinction.

Although not as accurately tabulated as the loss of human lives, the story of lost wildlife—of animals trapped in wildfires and birds navigating our contaminated skies—is equally horrifying. We'll never have accurate statistics for that loss. What we'll have is a professional and scientific estimate of loss for those creatures that live, for the most part, outside of our immediate range of vision.

So much pain. So much destruction. So much loss. I'm heartsick.

September 13, 2020

Six months ago today, I was a free agent. On March 13—Friday, the 13th—I shopped at Trader Joe's, stopped at the post office, got gas—the usual. After that day, and since that day, I have been in lockdown—sheltering in place—whatever the current terminology. I've been at home, exclusively.

I didn't know on that day that I wouldn't be going out again. It became clear in the next few days, as the state shut down. If only the state had maintained that shutdown, we wouldn't be in the sorry state we're in today. The case and death rates have leveled off and declined somewhat, but many Californians do not/will not accept that the pandemic is still with us. We should post signs at every corner: "Danger: Stay Inside."

Now, with wildfires still consuming millions of acres in this and neighboring states, the sky continues to be gray, gloomy, overcast. It is not overwhelmingly hot, as it was over Labor Day weekend, but there is no temptation to go outside, to walk, exercise, breathe in the fresh air. There is no fresh air. The air, already contaminated with disease, is now contaminated with the smoky residue of multiple out-of-control wildfires. I hear the words "existential crisis" more often than I ever have before. Our world—our global environment—is sick, wounded, gasping.

Six months, and no end in sight. No blue skies, no fluffy white clouds, no morning air so fresh and fragrant it pulls me outside no matter my schedule or my plans. September in southern California can be brutally hot, but there's the promise of cool evenings ahead.

There is no promise in the air today. The hostile air, the shadowless light, is ominous. I am in a dark place.

September 16, 2020

Global cases: 29,620,800
Global deaths: 935,900

US cases: 6,624,575
US deaths: 196,058

⌣‿⌒

These are not cold statistics. These are unique and irreplaceable women and men whose lives have been severed, suddenly and with no reprieve. With global deaths from Covid-19 approaching one million, and deaths here in the U.S. approaching 200,000, it's difficult to comprehend the enormity of the loss. And yet each of those individuals is mourned by his or her circle of family and friends. Each man and woman leaves a void in the community and in the particular temporal space he or she inhabited. Each one is missed.

⌣‿⌒

Today, *The Guardian* reported thousands of birds "falling out of the sky" and dying in the southwestern United States, including New Mexico, Colorado, Texas, Arizona, and Nebraska. Hundreds of thousands of birds could be dead already. The species include flycatchers, swallows, and warblers. Biologists speculate that "historic" wildfires across the western United States could have forced the birds to "re-route" their migration and move inland, where food and water are scarce.

In other words, they starved to death in the course of a migration that is as essential to them as flight itself.

⌣‿⌒

I am in mourning. For the human life lost. For the wildlife we often forget in the midst of personal concerns. For our burning and flooding and melting environment—our scarred and devastated world.

September 21, 2020

Rest in peace, RBG.

It's Monday. Ruth Bader Ginsburg—the "Notorious RBG" —died on Friday. She will lie in state in the Capitol—the first woman to be so honored.

There's a vicious Supreme Court power grab going on in the Republican Party, headed by Mitch McConnell and, of course, Donald Trump.

RBG's last request, as noted by her granddaughter, was as follows:

> *My most fervent wish is that I will not be replaced until a new president is installed.*

I heard the news of RBG's death on Friday afternoon. Seven hours later, almost to the minute, a 4.5-magnitude earthquake woke me up from a sound sleep. I heard things tumbling off shelves in the living room. I got up, checked for damage (there was none), noted the time (11:40 p.m.), texted my family, and went back to bed.

September 22, 2020

Meantime, depending on the statistical source chosen, and the media consulted, we surpassed 200,000 U.S. deaths somewhere between the 19th and today—a number that seemed inconceivable earlier this year.

I'm thinking back to the day *The New York Times* published the names and a brief bio of 1,000 of the first 100,000 Americans who died from Covid-19. The date was Sunday, May 24. The headline referred to "an incalculable loss."

That was four months ago.

Today, the number of U.S. deaths is within a few thousand of the number of people who live in many typical mid-sized American communities. At the current death rate of about 1,000 deaths per day, we'll reach that number—and then surpass it—soon.

September 27, 2020

It was early morning, not long after sunrise. Louise sat beneath her pink patio umbrella, on a pink wrought iron chair, pulled close to a white table with the umbrella stand plunged through its center. She reached for her mug of black coffee and her iPhone.

It was cool, breezy. The heat had not yet set in, so she could tolerate being outside; she could enjoy the newly visible day. She sipped her mug of coffee as she glanced through the news on her cell phone. She was wearing navy blue shorts and a loose cotton top, pale blue, soft and grayish from innumerable washings; sandals on her feet; nothing binding; nothing hindering; no makeup, except for lip gloss. Her hair, grayish blonde, growing by about an inch a month, was brushed away from her face, held in place by a white clip. Although she preferred short hair, it was a minor inconvenience. There were so many minor inconveniences in her life, none of which mattered. All that mattered, it seemed, was the news—an endless array of stories about mendacity—each with its headline-shouting insinuations, accusations, glaring pronouncements.

For a moment, her thoughts turned to the source of the word that seemed to her so appropriate to the news stories: mendacity. What was the line she was trying to remember? Ah, yes. It was from *Cat on a Hot Tin Roof.* Brick says to Big Daddy, "Mendacity is the system we live in." For a few moments, she thought about mendacity, about Brick, Big Daddy, Maggie the Cat, the repugnant Pollitts—inspired surname. It made her feel better, somehow. Literary connections helped to keep her grounded, to put the random chaos of the here and now in some sort of context.

She could hear her neighbors' muffled voices—in the apartment building behind her; from the house next door, where someone in the back yard of her quiet Silver Lake neighborhood was talking excitedly on a cell phone. She could see an elderly couple strolling past her on the sidewalk a few yards from where she sat, both wearing a mask; a young woman, masked, walking her pug; a boy (no mask) on a bicycle; a chattering toddler holding tight to his mother's hand while she listened, not to him, but to someone on the cell phone she held to her ear. Neither wore a mask.

Her patio was private but not hidden, a tiled and fenced-in sanctuary outside her small detached cottage, separated from the street by a grassy incline. The little fountain near her study window regurgitated its infinitely replenished waterfall. A sparrow splashed joyfully in its basin. Hummingbirds attacked each other to get at the feeder hanging a few feet away. The air whispered against her hair, against her skin. She was comfortable and yet—her eyes kept going back to the news. She glanced at the book that lay closed on the table. It was *Pale Horse, Pale Rider*, the latest book club selection. She meant to page through it again, but she sat on, sipping her coffee, glancing at headlines, doing as little as possible.

Of course, she would be punished for sitting on her terrace for any length of time, on this brightening day, late September but still summer in southern California. The punishment would be severe: raised red welts on her skin, where virtually invisible insects—called, by fellow victims, "No-See-Ums"—had attacked and left their itchy inscriptions on her ankles, her thighs, her arms, the patch of skin where her shirt and her shorts parted company. The female of the species—a microscopic fly—pierced the skin with its four minuscule cutting blades, extracted the blood needed to reproduce, then flew away to lay its eggs.

But the morning was, after all, so beautiful. The sky, somewhat blue after weeks of hazy gray brought on by the wildfires, was not the striking blue she associated with September, but a washed-out blue, like her shirt. The air was moderately unhealthy. In a few hours, the heat would be intolerable. So she sat on, sipping her coffee, glancing at her cell phone, avoiding her book. She sat on, although she wanted not to be here, not to be so intractably where she was.

She wanted to be a young girl again, her life in front of her instead of behind her. She wanted to have hope, that excess of optimism that is the very essence of youth. What was there to look forward to? What was in her weather forecast? What was her usefulness to those she loved but with whom she could not share a room, a physical space? Her life, like the fountain, gushed up each day, then plummeted down into the basin where, after a brief interval, it gushed up again. The same water, the same trajectory, the same choice—turn it on or turn it off.

Outside, beyond her small enclosure, her limited universe, her safe haven, was a country in confusion, grappling with wildly distorted messages, with more than 200,000 lives lost to a pandemic tragically exacerbated by political mayhem. Politics raged, all-consuming, like the California wildfires. There was no tamping it down, no escape except to contain it, to inhibit its destructive effects.

She had no children from her failed marriage, but her sister had provided her with two nieces and two nephews, now adults. They were scattered, but she had always been physically present in their lives. She missed the drama of their loud, random, self-involved lifestyles—the daily, hourly tragicomedy. It couldn't be duplicated on FaceTime and Zoom. She couldn't replicate their importance to her on a digital device, nor could she find the reassurance she longed for—of *her* importance to *them*.

For now, she could not move outside of her limited orbit. She could not reach out, except virtually. There was only this endless cycle of days, in which the hours ticked on without substantial change, substantial progress. It was not Hell. It was not Purgatory. It was Limbo.

And the lies swirled around her. They were invisible but, like the No-See-Ums, they were everywhere. She and everyone in this toxic environment were being battered with lies, pierced by the cutting blades of mendacity—leaving behind swollen red patches of unbearably itchy flesh.

October 7, 2020

The presidential debate on Tuesday, September 29, made me queasy, drained me physically—as though I were attempting a marathon without previous training—and left me psychically stunned. I have never witnessed such brazen contempt for norms, such disregard of everyone and everything within the president's orbit, including the television audience. The president came onto the stage looking disheveled, high-colored, angry, and hostile. His mouth never turned up in the ensuing 90 minutes. He was angry and hostile from beginning to end. Joe Biden fought continually to be heard, to complete a thought. The interruptions were continual, contemptuous, merciless—a maelstrom of verbal shotgun projectiles designed to bring down the quarry with volume rather than with accuracy. I wanted to turn it off, but I didn't. I felt an obligation to stay with Biden while he was under attack.

Then, on Thursday, October 1, I learned that the president and the first lady had tested positive for Covid-19. I waited up with Brian Williams on MSNBC for the confirmation he was obviously waiting for. He got it—on October 2 at 1:00 a.m. ET; on October 1 at 10:00 p.m. my time.

And the "unreality show" (my term) continued—with the usual commercial breaks—right up to this moment, with the president hospitalized at Walter Reed Army Medical Center, helicoptered to and from the hospital, after three days, to walk up the stairs of the White House and stand, Mussolini-like, on the Truman balcony trying to look presidential, but—orange-faced, saucer-haired, fighting for breath—looking more like a comic-book villain.

Since then, like bowling pins, his aides have been tumbling down with the virus, although the number has grown far beyond the regulation ten-pins. In addition, several Joint Chiefs of Staff have gone into quarantine.

Apparently, the "superspreader" event was the White House celebration of Amy Coney Barrett's nomination to the Supreme Court (to replace Ruth Bader Ginsburg). The outdoor event took place on Saturday, September 26, and was attended by at least 200 guests sitting close together in the White House Rose Garden, followed by hugging, kissing, and fist bumping, both indoors and out.

Amy Coney Barrett was accompanied by her husband and their seven children, aged eight to 19, all of whom sat in the same front row with the first lady who, a few days later, tested positive for Covid-19. The children also interacted with the president indoors (as shown in photos) after the event.

Neither the first lady, the Supreme Court nominee, her husband, nor their seven children wore masks. After the event, the children went back to school, potentially exposing others to infection.

The September 26 superspreader event was followed, the next day, by the disclosure, in *The New York Times*, of the president's tax records and tax evasions for the past twenty years.

This was followed, on Tuesday, September 29, by the infamous debate.

The VP, Mike Pence, is apparently still upright and will debate Kamala Harris tonight, from behind Plexiglass screens. I'm surprised the Biden campaign agreed to it. Zoom would be a much better format for engaging with the overwhelmingly infested Trump staff.

I'll just mention, for historical purposes, that during the Pence/Harris debate, a fly—about to be famous in its own right—landed on Mike Pence's hair. Black fly on white hair. Impossible to miss. Impossible to look away. The fly settled in for several minutes, after which it departed, an anonymous insect once again, as unaware of its moment of fame as was the VP of its presence atop his head. It was an unexpected but welcome gift of humor enjoyed by social media, late-night hosts, and Democrats everywhere.

October 13, 2020

Today, Tuesday, three weeks before election day, seven months to the day after I began sheltering in place, I voted.

My ballot is filled in, signed, sealed, dated, ready to go. Tomorrow, I'll take my ballot to a drop box less than a mile from my home. I've taken photos of my ballot and the envelope and signed up for follow-my-vote messages. I have no trust in or respect for the current administration. Vote tracking makes sense.

Today, in preparation for this momentous event, I cleaned my car windows with Windex, a squeegee, and a lot of paper towels. I had to go around the car twice to get through the black dirt to the windows beneath. Is this the air we breathe when we go outside?

Today is vote day. Tomorrow will be ballot-box day.

October 14, 2020

I dropped off my ballot today. I went to my community library parking lot, where a ballot box has been installed behind the book drop. No one was there when I drove up, so I parked crossways, close to the box, wearing a mask. As I dropped my ballot in the box, another car drove up. The gray-haired woman who got out of the car, ballot in hand, was not wearing a mask. I got out of her way as quickly as I could.

I went from there to my neighborhood gas station, where I filled up my almost-empty gas tank for the first time in months.

It's like coming out of hibernation—first I yawn and stretch, then I look around, then I rouse myself and saunter outside into the "real" world, hesitant and fearful—where people seem to be taking precautions when and how they please.

October 15, 2020

As of today, per the Johns Hopkins University Coronavirus Resource Center, the number of deaths attributed to Covid-19 is 217,745, while confirmed cases in the U.S. (7,974,502) are approaching eight million.

I'm listening to and watching a lot of news these days, and I often hear those who have died from Covid-19 referred to as "lost souls." This reference—which, by the way, I've used myself—can be misleading. These are not lost souls; these are lost bodies, lost lives. Their souls—and I believe we have souls—exist in another dimension: the dimension of faith, the dimension of memory, the dimension of legacy.

If I die of this virus, I hope my soul is not "lost." I hope it lives on—in the memories of my family and friends, in my books and other writings, in whatever afterlife is available to me.

I am a non-practicing Catholic, made up of equal parts faith, doubt, and skepticism. Is there a "life" after death? My religious background says "Yes." The Notre Dame nuns who taught me in grade school say "Yes." The Jesuits who taught me as an undergraduate say "Yes."

I say, "I don't know. Maybe. Probably not."

I may be a lost soul in life—but not in death. In death, I will be loved by a few, remembered with affection by a few more, forgotten by most. My soul—that which is me and no one else—will, with faith, live on in some timeless parallel universe inhabited by other souls and a Creator with neither male nor female attributes. Without faith, my soul will linger for a while, and then—along with my body—become a part of the infinite substance of the universe.

Notable quotes:

"A bureaucrat defending an autocrat"
Source: Phillip Halpern, former Assistant U.S.
    Attorney, in reference to Attorney General Bill Barr
    and President Trump (MSNBC).

"What does that look like?"
Source: Everyone. Everywhere. This particular phrase
    has been transmitted throughout the media like
    the virus itself. I dislike it—perhaps because it has
    become virus-like in its spread.

Forecast:

This is what Halloween and Thanksgiving will "look like" for my family and me.

Halloween will be a non-event. I'll buy candy for the neighborhood kiddies, put the candy—each piece wrapped and sealed—on the porch in my Halloween spider bowl. As I won't be monitoring, I'll hope that the little kids get their fair share before the big kids arrive.

Possible alternative: I will not buy candy. I will not answer the door if they call out, "Trick or treat!" in their adorable little-kid voices. I'll hope for understanding in re the "trick."

I'll FaceTime with the family or get photos—perhaps a video—of the boys in their Halloween costumes.

On Thanksgiving, my son or daughter-in-law will bring me a covered platter with all sorts of dinner delicacies.

He or she will greet me from a distance and hand over the goodies. I, in turn, will present him or her with a pie—probably apple.

Possible alternative: They will drive here with the boys in the back seat. They will park close to the front door. The boys will greet me from the back seat, or on the sidewalk, wearing their masks. They will wave, throw kisses, shout, "Happy Thanksgiving!" We will do the food exchange, as above.

I miss my family.

October 21, 2020

Charlie was the first to respond to Sybil's "How are you?" as the book club gathered for its Zoom meeting. Theresa and Louise were busy adjusting themselves and their computer screens inside their familiar rectangles.

"I feel like a hamster going round and round on that little wheel thing—sure as hell it's going somewhere but always ending up in the same place."

"This whole year has been like riding a hamster wheel, Charlie," said Sybil.

"Joan says I'm driving her crazy," Charlie went on. "I spend most of my time here in my playroom—even when I'm not working. The boys are busy doing their antisocial thing—online games, mostly, when it's not online elementary school. Even Fido is off his food."

"It won't be long now," said Sybil, "till we know the outcome of the vote. Then, at least, we'll know who's in charge."

"I'm counting the days," Charlie replied.

"Meantime, we're reading *Pale Horse, Pale Rider*," said Louise. "Thanks for the suggestion, Theresa."

Theresa nodded. "Well, nobody wanted to read *The Great Influenza*—even though Bill Gates put it on his pandemic reading list—so I thought we'd try a fictional take on the 1918 wartime pandemic."

"All wrapped up in a love story," said Sybil. "Delicious."

Charlie tried to look attentive as Theresa took up the discussion and went on—*droned on*, thought Charlie—about Katherine Anne Porter's insisting on its being called a "short novel" and not a "novella," but his eyes kept wandering off-screen, taking in his self-designated "playroom," where he worked—far more than he played—as a film editor. The room faced the fenced back yard of their Craftsman house in West Hollywood, where he could see his two young boys rigorously exercising Fido, and themselves, as they threw a Frisbee to each other. Fido, never discouraged, ran back and forth, leaping for the Frisbee, which the boys kept just out of reach.

Charlie's playroom was the house's blueprint "study," far enough away from the kitchen and living room to be relatively quiet. One wall was lined with bookshelves, the shelves filled with film reels, video cassettes, CDs, DVDs, books, and files, in no special order. His desk was crowded with a laptop, three side-by-side monitors, books and papers, a blizzard of Post-It notes. Charlie liked an overall appearance of casual disorder, but he could locate items instantly. Sybil's spotless kitchen and Theresa's Victorian-perfect living room made him tense, uncomfortable.

Charlie had painted two sides of the playroom blue and one side green. Behind the wall of bookshelves was a faux-brick wall, which he had left untouched when he and Joan moved in years before.

Although he knew he was perceived as somewhat lowbrow, Charlie read widely and thought deeply about matters that concerned him. He liked knowing that he could surpass expectations. He assured his book club friends that understanding him was just a matter of decoding his sometimes-muddled remarks and ignoring his dorky attempts at humor. Louise, Theresa, and Sybil had done just that and, over the years, had accepted him as an important quadrant of their small circle.

"'There's too much of everything in the world just now.'"

Sybil's voice brought him to attention.

"I think that's the most important line in *Pale Horse, Pale Rider*. It sums up the story, and it sums up what's happening in our world right now. We have the pandemic, the election, the economy, the Black Lives Matter movement, and a continual stream of venom and lies from our president. Miranda and her young man, Adam, have the 1918 pandemic and World War I. He's a soldier in the army and about to be shipped overseas. They're enjoying their last few days together."

Sybil found a marked passage in her book.

"To quote again from the story, because Katherine Anne Porter says it so well, they're enjoying 'the simple and lovely miracle of being two persons named Adam and Miranda, twenty-four years old each, alive and on the earth at the same moment.'"

Charlie dove into the discussion, reading from his underlined and notated copy of the book.

"Adam knows he'll probably die, either under fire or because of the pandemic. He talks about men 'dying like flies' from this 'funny new disease.' Miranda responds that it 'seems to be' a plague, 'something out of the Middle Ages.' They're walking down the street and they stop to watch a funeral procession pass by."

Charlie paused, then added, "They're surrounded by death, and trying their damndest to play it cool."

Theresa spoke up.

"Eventually, of course, Adam does die, not in action but from the plague—which he catches from Miranda, who almost dies. He takes care of her until she's hospitalized."

"Were they any more aware of the perils of the pandemic than we are today?" asked Louise.

"It didn't seem to be a political issue," said Charlie. "It was a given—like the war. They didn't seem to be taking precautions. Maybe they were practicing what Trump calls 'herd mentality' and the rest of the world calls herd immunity."

"So," said Sybil, "it's history repeating itself, though perhaps not line for line."

Charlie spoke up again.

"What I like about this story is it puts me right smack in the 1918 mindset. I can feel the uncertainty, the fear, the acceptance, the determination to live for the moment. Adam's expectation is that he will die; Miranda is pushing on out of sheer will, choosing to love rather than to give up hope. They're carrying on under the double whammy of war and a pandemic."

Theresa's screen lit up as she began to speak. A teacher both in experience and by inclination, she could seldom resist a summation.

"Maybe that's what we can learn from the story," she said. "When we're in the middle of a global crisis, we think nothing as bad has ever happened before. But, of course, it has. We just have to look backward to find something similar."

She looked down at her desk, picked up a handwritten note.

"It was called the Spanish flu—most likely a misnomer. It lasted from February 1918 to April 1920. It infected 500 million people—about a quarter of the world's population at the time—in four successive waves."

She glanced up.

"We're in the third wave of the pandemic right now."

She read again from her note.

"Death estimates vary—a conservative estimate is 50 million people. To put that in context, there were about 17 million military and civilian deaths during the first World War."

She paused—*for effect*, Charlie thought—before she concluded.

"In October 1918, alone, nearly 200,000 Americans died. The U.S. death total was about 675,000."

She looked up.

"Sound familiar?"

There were groans and overlapping responses from the Zoom screens.

"We know so much more now," said Sybil. "We shouldn't be mirroring that century-old tragic event so exactly."

"Katherine Anne Porter did what good novelists do so well," said Louise. "She told us the story from the point of view of two people in love, who are clinging to their last few days together in a world that is sick and at war. She puts this period in American life in context, gives it flesh and blood and bones. It's why we read fiction."

Charlie nodded his assent but said nothing as the discussion went on. He looked out of his window again, to check on the boys. They were examining Fido's paw. One of them had stomped on it, or perhaps Fido had stepped on a bee. The dog was squirming and wriggling, but the two boys held him fast.

Hold on, he said, muttering the words as he watched the boys. *Hold on, Charlie. Got to make this work. Got to make my life work. Got to make Joan and me work. Hold on.*

He shook his head, as if to clear it, just as Fido jumped out of reach and sped away.

Can't control a goddamned thing, he thought. *Tired of it all. Tired. Where's Joan?*

Just then, he heard Joan's voice and saw her walk outside from the kitchen, looking young and seductive in shorts, halter, flip-flops, her ponytail swinging. She was questioning the boys, who were on the defensive. She pointed toward the house; the boys meekly walked inside, their heads down, their unspoken sentiment obvious.

Hey, it's not our fault! Mom's always on our case.

Joan glanced toward the window, flashed him a grin, mimicked a strut.

She keeps me going, he thought. *I've got to make more of an effort—help out more. While she's still there for me.*

He'd lost one wife—didn't pay attention till she walked out on him. He was too old to start over again—nearly half a century behind him, no room in his life for another disaster—not when there were kids involved.

My fault, mostly, this void between Joan and me. She keeps us going; she keeps the Frisbee up in the air; I'm the one who lets it drop.

He thought back, to the months before the pandemic, when the book club members were still meeting at each other's homes, when he had stepped out of his book club role and stepped into a role he had no right to assume—that of Sybil's confidant when she was struggling through a marital crisis. Nothing had happened, but it could have, as he well knew.

I'm a selfish bastard. Took advantage of her, of Sybil, when she was most vulnerable. It's okay now, I think, but it was close. Too close. Good thing we're locked up.

"What do you think, Charlie?" asked Louise.

"About what?"

Charlie turned away from the window and focused on the computer screen.

"Where have you been?" she said, laughing. "We're going to continue our discussion next time. It's a good story, don't you agree?"

"Like you said," he replied, "it's why we read fiction."

October 28, 2020

Full disclosure: I've become a news junkie during the months I've been sheltering in place. Even now, as I write this, I'm listening to the news, intent on the pandemic and the election coming up next Tuesday, November 3.

As the CDC has, with this administration, lost its credibility, I periodically check out alternate sources for current pandemic statistics. I haven't figured out which source my go-to news channel (NBC/MSNBC) is using, so I look around, always finding disparity. The CDC is always low; NBC/MSNBC is always high. That's the only analysis I've been able to make. It may be because, among other lapses, the CDC isn't updating as regularly as are other sources.

U.S. Deaths
225,985 (CDC)
227,177 (Johns Hopkins)
227,235 (The New York Times)
228,371 (NBC)

The election is impossible to predict, especially since there's undoubtedly a lot of hanky-panky both planned and in process surrounding the vote count. I'm encouraged by the pre-election-day vote, but apprehensive regarding Trump's ability to step down, and the actual as well as potential violence being triggered by his messaging.

October 29, 2020

Trump is transparent. He can't get enough praise—as his need is limitless—so he adds to the measure with incessant self-aggrandizement.

One of the most obvious examples of this pathetic need is his constant use of the word "Sir" in reference to himself.

He can't get enough of calling himself "Sir." In every anecdote in his vast store of flattering anecdotes, the person addressing him—without exception—repeats the word "Sir" multiple times.

"And then he said to me, Sir, he said, Sir, is it true, Sir, that ..."

The "Sirs" go on, to the end of the anecdote. *He can't say it enough.* The fact that he is a "Sir" is paramount in his mind—seemingly more important than anything he is referencing.

Perhaps he believes that, if he repeats the "Sir" enough times, people listening will more easily accept his authority, or he himself will come to believe in and accept his own position of authority. A man has to be monumentally insecure to require this amount of reassurance.

The Trump ego is like an enormous but leaky balloon that requires a constant infusion of hot air.

November 2, 2020

Even at this late date, I remain cautiously optimistic. However, I fear violence. I fear chaos instigated by an unhinged would-be autocrat who will not admit defeat. It will take an overwhelming victory to tamp down Trump's obvious itch to incite his followers. A significant number of those tens of thousands who show up at his rallies are devotees in the most radical sense. They will do whatever he signals them to do—and they're waiting for those signals, guns at the ready.

A few days ago, he applauded the headline-making assault on a Biden/Harris campaign bus in Texas. Trump supporters in trucks surrounded the bus on a Texas highway, waving Trump flags and almost running the bus off the road. Trump retweeted part of the video and wrote "I LOVE TEXAS!" with his usual all-caps emphasis. What's next, with that kind of blatant encouragement?

After five unremitting years of Donald Trump, I wonder: who is he, anyway? Through some fluke, some ill-fated convergence of events, he became President of the United States of America in 2016. Tomorrow, hopefully, America will undertake the process of demoting him to his pre-2015 status as reality show celebrity, bankrupt real estate developer, and private citizen.

An estimated 100 million Americans will have already cast their vote before tomorrow's election day. They'll be counted, along with election day and mail-in votes, tomorrow and in the days following. Trump wants to declare victory tomorrow night and call a halt to the count. He won't halt the process, but he will alert his cult followers that it's time for all hell to break loose. Anything could happen in the days and weeks following.

If he loses, Trump will have almost three months—from November 4 to January 20—to crash and burn everything around him. He can do a lot of damage in those eleven weeks. Seventy-seven days to smash whatever vestiges of government he has left intact. Eleven weeks to pardon himself and his cronies for their unfettered carnage. Seventy-seven days to destroy damaging evidence. Eleven weeks to use the podium of power to beat his chest and roar out his anger and indignation. Seventy-seven days to call on that 42 to 45 percent of the voting public who will continue to adore him, support him, do his bidding—whether coded or brazenly open in its messaging.

My take on the guy? He's a sociopath; therefore, he has no conscience, no empathy, and no consideration for anyone outside of his limited sphere. He's a con man; therefore, he's never offstage—even when the stage is empty and the audience is gone. He needs to believe in his own potency in order to exist. He's a realtor because his father was a realtor and groomed him for the job; therefore, he must persist as a businessman, creating his own success story despite multiple bankruptcies and substantial financial loss. He's an elected president; therefore, he cannot admit to a second-term defeat without, at the same time, admitting to failure.

Most of all, he's a product—and I use that word deliberately—of a career in reality TV. Television is his reality. Reality television is his métier, the stage for his most spectacular success, the theater in which he feels most secure, most applauded, most successful.

Unfortunately, he aimed higher than TV stardom. He turned his sights to the ultimate power center—politics. His ambition: to enlarge his audience, to be a world-class celebrity, a reality star without peer. In a way, he achieved this ambition. He will go down in history as an unprecedented presidential phenomenon—never before matched in terms of corruption, manipulation, ignorance, and flagrant abuse of power.

He was ultimately impeached by the House of Representatives in 2019. Does anyone remember this? He seems to have forgotten it. Many of us remember it as a hugely satisfying process that took place many ages ago. Most likely, his followers have come to view it as a badge of honor, if they remember it at all.

Now, as Trump himself says, it's "Covid, Covid, Covid." He wants it to go away, but he's holding multiple rallies with thousands of followers cheering him on, maskless, packed close together. There are now, in the U.S., close to 100,000 new Covid cases recorded each day, with 1,000 deaths per day, while Trump—live and in person—addresses cheering crowds in states with soaring case rates. He's ignoring the pandemic crisis, denigrating Dr. Anthony Fauci, the government's top infectious disease authority—threatening to fire him—allowing his frantic following to chant "Fire Fauci" at rallies. The pandemic haunts him, but he refuses to acknowledge it as a threat—even after he, his wife, his 14-year-old son, and multiple White House personnel contracted the virus. He's in permanent denial, as are those who attend his current reality show: The Donald Trump Rally.

Who is he, anyway? He's a reality show celebrity who leaped into politics with no credentials except for his name recognition and his brash and brazen attacks on his competition. And here I am, the day before Election Day 2020, hoping for a voter turnout that will reject all he stands for, and restore sanity to the administration of our government—so that we can control the pandemic, heal the environment, restore normalcy to the economy, and—most of all—get rid of the pestilence in the White House.

Of course, I've said this before and I must say it again—we'll never get rid of him. He'll steal headlines until the day he dies; his family members will wave the Trump banner when he no longer can. History will carry his story of the misuse of power down through the years. Our only option is to contain him and relegate him to a place outside of the citadels of power.

He'll have television—perhaps his own version of Fox network—with no dissenting voices. He'll have whatever is left of his real estate holdings when the legal proceedings have run their course. He'll have a library of books, movies, and documentaries attempting to dissect and understand him and his political dominance. He'll have the recognition of historians as they present him to future generations, while binding him inextricably to the pandemic he has chosen to trivialize and ignore.

Who is he, anyway? From all I've read and heard about him, he was, and remains to this day, a small, insecure boy whose father didn't love him enough, who is terrified of the one thing his father would never allow, would never forgive, would never understand. His father taught him the one lesson that has followed him, haunted him, throughout his seven decades of life. There are only two options: winning or losing. If you win, you're successful. If you lose, you're not just a failure—you're an object of ridicule. You're beneath contempt.

Donald Trump Defeated is what we have to look forward to. The consequence of that defeat is what we have to dread.

November 3, 2020

It's Election Day.

3:30 p.m.

I feel prickly. Anticipation mixed with equal parts hope and fear. The lines at the polls are not long, which is reassuring, because Trump and others predicted tens of thousands of voters would be surging to the polls today, per Trump's directive. Pray God, with 100 million votes cast before today, Biden is already firmly in the lead. Any other outcome is unthinkable.

5:30 p.m.

Excruciating. States going to Trump. Florida up in the air but tending toward Trump. Trump and Mitch McConnell win in Kentucky. Trump wins Tennessee. Biden wins Washington, D.C.

8:00 p.m.

I'm listening/watching MSNBC on my iPhone while doing mindless tasks at my desk. The analysts seem demoralized. I hear in their voices what I'm feeling. Right now, the electoral votes are 192/114. Biden leads, but he just got California's 55 electoral votes. Nothing seems to be changing from 2016. How can that be? We know these men; one is a good man; the other is corrupt. Why is the vote so close? Why are voters rousingly voting a corrupt man back in? It's unfathomable.

Chyron/news crawl/news ticker:

Tight race may come down to PA, MI, WI, AZ & NC

8:30 p.m.

An analyst just called a possible Arizona win for Biden as "the revenge of John McCain." Florida seems a lost cause. Let Trump have his adopted state. We can win without it.

11:30 p.m.

I'm done with him. He's speaking now, claiming a premature victory, unwilling to wait for the vote tabulation. The election is "off," he says. He's claiming victory with states that have not yet finished their count. With very little early and absentee votes counted, he's shedding doubt on the count. "We're going to protect the integrity of the vote," says Pence, softening his master's voice somewhat. "We're on the road to victory."

And off they go, having gutted the whole election process. What a fraud! Millions of votes have not yet been counted and Trump has called a halt to the process. Let's delegitimize this election, with Biden's 220 electoral votes, and Trump's 213. As far as Trump is concerned, he has won—in addition to Texas—Pennsylvania, Georgia, North Carolina, Michigan, etc. As far as he's concerned, the election is over and done with.

If there is an upset for Trump, he'll take it to the Supreme Court, with his handpicked Justice Amy Coney Barrett, as well as Neil Gorsuch and Brett Kavanaugh.

I can't do another four years of this. My imperfect heart won't take it.

November 4, 2020

It's the day after the day of.

1:00 p.m.

So-called "poll observers" have made their way inside the poll-counting headquarters at the TCF Center in Detroit, causing the expected chaos. Like any national or international extremists, these cult members have been given their march-ing orders and are carrying them out. There's no knowing what will follow, on a local basis as well as in the courts, where Trump will pursue his baseless claims right up to the Supreme Court.

My God, we're about to be inundated with images of Rudy Giuliani again. As the president's personal lawyer, he'll be doing his fatuous best to defend his boss.

Current electoral vote count: Biden 237/Trump 214.

1:10 p.m.

Joe Biden is speaking at this moment. He's announcing a win in WI by 20,000 votes, MI leading by 30,000 votes, PA by 78 percent of mail-in votes, a "flipped" AZ and NC, and so far a popular vote lead of 3 million. *"This is a major achievement."* He's not claiming victory, but he's anticipating it, saying, *"We will not be bullied."*

He ended with a thematic campaign statement: *"There will be no blue states and red states when we win—only the United States of America."*

1:26 p.m.

From Michigan, a win of 16 electoral votes: 253 for Biden; 214 for Trump.

Thank you, God—and Michigan.

3:00 p.m.

Joe Biden is projected winner of Michigan, "apparent" winner of Wisconsin.

4:30 p.m.

I feel as though a gigantic weight is being lifted off my shoulders—slowly. It's still weighing me down, but less so than an hour ago, much less so than last night, when I felt all was lost. I was wakeful last night, sleeping fitfully, waking up to check the news every few hours. I feel able to take a deep breath today, to breathe out with relief. I'm waking up from a four-year ordeal that is now, hopefully, behind us.

There's going to be a lot of conflict ahead; it has, in fact, already started, with lawsuits attempting to stop the count! But, if we make it to 270, we'll make it all the way.

Georgia is 16 electoral votes. That would take us to 269. That weight is still there. I feel it against my neck, between my shoulder blades. The waiting is hard.

5:30 p.m.

Joe Biden is ahead in popular votes by more than 3.5 million.

Biden	71,366,228
Trump	67,858,005

5:45 p.m.

MSNBC news ticker:

Trump campaign files lawsuits in MI, PA & GA

November 6, 2020

9:50 a.m.

The mayor of Philadelphia just advised Trump to *"put his big boy pants on"* and accept the fact that Biden has won in Pennsylvania.

I don't think I slept at all last night. I had my iPhone close by and, at 3:00 a.m., I tuned in to Morning Joe on MSNBC and listened/half-listened for the next four hours, slept a couple of hours, and got up about 8:45.

6:00 p.m.

I just heard this period in time called an "interregnum" by an MSNBC host. It's a good description of these strange, indecisive days, "a period when normal government is suspended," according to the dictionary.

At the same time, the coronavirus continues its stealthy surge. The daily count today is 123,695 new cases.

The popular vote:

    Biden   74,288,812
    Trump   70,156,781

A quote I just heard on my iPhone: *"For Trump, attention is oxygen."* Didn't catch the source.

8:00 p.m.

Joe Biden just now: *"We're going to win this race."*

Re Trump: *"We may be adversaries but we're not enemies."*

The speech was very brief—about five minutes. More to come soon, I hope.

November 7, 2020

Mission accomplished!

8:25 a.m.

Biden 279/Trump 214

Joe Biden is President of the United States of America.

I'm crying. I can't stop crying.

One of my favorite early messages, from the Mayor of Paris:

"Welcome back, America."

1:30 p.m.

A poem someone just recited, by Seamus Heaney, includes the lines, "... once in a lifetime/The longed-for tidal wave/Of justice can rise up ..."

This is a favorite Joe Biden poem, which I heard recited moments after he was elected 46th President of the United States of America.

When I heard the news, the feelings of relief, thankfulness, exhilaration, joy, were overwhelming. I had been waiting to exhale for months. Now, at last, we as a nation could do just that.

The street and neighborhood celebrations throughout the country show me how many of us feel as I did and do. I realize that, while 75 million people feel as I do, 70 million do not. More than 70 million people in these United States are not celebrating, are sad in the way I've been—so many of us have been—for the last four years. Hopefully, we can find a way to come together, at least to some degree.

I believe in the two-party system. I think the Republican *laissez faire* policy and the Democratic leanings toward socialism are a good balance. Since the Trump entrance in 2015, the Republican ethos has deteriorated, but it's still in its essence viable. I hope we return to an era in which both parties engage in a fair fight for ascendancy.

2:20 p.m.

Rev. Al Sharpton—the "Rev"—speaking "as a preacher" on MSNBC, said this about President-Elect Biden and Vice

President-Elect Harris: "God probably created both of them for this moment in time."

3:55 p.m.

Michael Beschloss, presidential historian, reflects on what might have happened if today had turned out differently: Trump in power for four more years, no reelection to worry about, even fewer reasons for constraint, conservative courts, Republican Senate. Closing caution: "Eternal vigilance is always the price of liberty."

4:25 p.m.

Political analyst: "We've had four years of a joyless presidency."

Psalm 30:5

For his anger endureth but a moment; in his favour is life: weeping may endure for a night, but joy cometh in the morning.

And joy did, indeed, come—at 8:25 this morning.

November 13, 2020

It's Friday the 13th—again.

11:15 a.m.

Breaking news re electoral votes:

> Biden 306 (including Georgia)
> Trump 232 (including North Carolina)

Trump's final electoral count in 2016: 306.

2:00 p.m.

A few minutes ago, Trump made a Rose Garden appearance, together with his "Warp Speed" team, to boast about his success with and take credit for the Pfizer vaccine and other supposed inroads in re Covid-19. It was his first public appearance in nine days. His words, demeanor, excesses, are the same as they were nine days ago. He has not relented— even though he almost said the word "next" in referring to the administration. He did not mention anything concerning the raging pandemic, the surging death rate, the unprecedented number of cases every one of us has witnessed in recent days. These statistics do not exist, as far as he's concerned.

> United States Covid-19 Statistics
> Cases: 10,693,773
> Deaths: 243,466

November 15, 2020

There is a tragic parallel in the current pandemic surge and Donald Trump's refusal to concede the election. Of course, they are inextricably connected, but it's more than that. We are, as a nation, at war with each other, in the same way we're at war with the pandemic. Although Joe Biden won the presidential election by more than five million votes, there are millions of citizens of this nation who, like Trump, are in complete denial of the coronavirus, and in profound disagreement with the election results. How are we to get past that? Can we get past it? Perhaps not.

Today, in a CNBC op-ed, Frederick Kempe quoted a 2007 interview with Donald Trump in the London *Observer*. Trump was asked, "If no one were looking at you, do you think you'd still exist?" Trump replied: "No. Because, honestly, I wouldn't have any fun. There are people who are successful, but nobody knows who they are, and I say what's the purpose? Everyone knows who I am."

Trump is a celebrity and a social phenomenon. He won't go away. He is not capable of going away. We're coming up with a vaccine for Covid-19 but, as I said in my first entry, on April 1, there is no Trump vaccine.

We are dealing with someone who, as he spends his last days teetering in place, knowing he must ultimately relinquish his position, is contemplating his very survival. If his existence is dependent on the perception of Donald Trump as a powerful public figure, he can't make a quiet and dignified withdrawal. That would mean he would no longer be seen and heard by all. He must, in terms of his own self-definition, be seen and heard by as many people as possible, even as the roots give way and he topples over.

If a tree falls in the forest and no one hears it, does it make a sound?

This old saw goes back to Dr. George Berkeley (1685–1753), Anglican bishop and philosopher. His answer was that God hears it, so it does make a sound.

My answer is that, *yes*, that tree does make a sound because human beings are not the only sentient creatures in the world—although we tend to ignore that fact. The sound of a falling tree is heard by wild animals, birds, even vibration-sensitive insects.

Donald Trump is not alone in his egotistical worldview. We, as humans, tend to disregard our close association with the non-human life that surrounds and sustains us. Wildlife is, literally as well as figuratively, falling all around us—in rainforest destruction, in Arctic melt, in deadly wildfires, in extreme weather events—fueled by energy consumption and production to meet our insatiable need for "progress" and ascendancy.

I don't feel sorry for Trump, but I do feel sorry for all of us as we face the existential threat of climate change, while dealing with a pandemic surge, a two-party political system whose participants are deaf to each other's views, and an egomaniac-in-charge with two months left to make as much noise as possible.

November 23, 2020

About the endless election.

3:30 p.m.

It took three weeks, but it finally happened—just minutes ago. The exquisitely branded General Services Administration (GSA) and Emily Murphy, its infamous Trump-appointed administrator, have given Joe Biden the transition go-ahead. He and his team will now have access to the information they should have had 16 days ago when, on Saturday morning, November 7, Joe Biden became the president-elect.

In order for the transition process to go forward from one presidency to the next, Murphy is required to sign a formal letter allowing the transition process to begin. She did not put pen to paper until today.

In a Trump tweet, the soon-to-be-ex-president took credit (as usual), giving the official go-ahead for the transition to a Biden administration.

If for no other reason, I would never open a Twitter account because Twitter has been indelibly stamped and stigmatized by Trump. Until January 20 at 12:00 noon ET, he is President of the United States of America. Could he not—between rounds of golf—find a better, more dignified venue for this and similarly important announcements and pronouncements?

Meanwhile, the pandemic continues on its relentless destructive path, while our contemporary Nero plays golf.

About the endless pandemic:

> Current United States Covid-19 Statistics
> Cases: 12,404,987
> Deaths: 257,616

I heard on the news this morning that more than two million travelers passed through flight checkpoint security lines this past weekend. Two million people are heading home for the Thanksgiving holiday. Two million people are potentially infecting and/or being infected by the Covid-19 coronavirus.

The CDC estimates that 40 percent of all coronavirus transmissions occur from people who show no symptoms. In addition, a person can test negative and, a day or two later—even hours later—can test positive. Our testing procedures are not a free pass. That trip may cost the traveler—and the traveler's friends and family—dearly.

November 25, 2020

Sybil stood in her sunny kitchen, with its white cabinets, stainless steel appliances, and the breakfast nook where she had set up her laptop, books, papers, and writing supplies. There were many other options for this arrangement in the spacious Pasadena house, but the nook was the only place where she felt comfortable, even somewhat "cozy."

It was time to get ready for the book club meeting on Zoom.

She hugged herself, rubbing the warmth of the afternoon sun into her upper arms. Even in the warmest weather, she often felt chilled in this house, where the temperature was kept at 70 degrees year-round.

"It's a good, moderate temperature," Greg had told her, when she first attempted to adjust the thermostat. "We set it for 70 when we moved in and never changed it after that."

The "we" invoked Andrea, Greg's first wife. Greg and Andrea had had the perfect union—until they didn't. She, Sybil, was the young and malleable replacement for a successful marriage disrupted by Andrea's infatuation with one of Greg's colleagues.

Sybil was approaching forty and not that young anymore, but she still felt as though she were in the student phase of being a successful internist's second wife, trying to fill the gap Andrea had left when she left him.

Andrea's "infatuation" had turned out to be enduring. She and the former colleague had married and lived in Phoenix now—so Sybil no longer had to fear she would run into her at Whole Foods, or Macy's, or CVS. But Andrea remained entrenched in the house, her DNA on every surface, and Greg would not move.

"It's a perfect house, in a great location" he had said, soothingly, when she brought up the subject during pillow talk. "It's our investment in the future. We couldn't duplicate it, even if we sank every cent of the sale into a new house."

"It's your past," she had responded, careful not to raise her voice. Greg disliked raised voices.

"Not anymore," he had replied, kissing her lightly. "It's *our* house now."

With that, he had turned his back on her, fluffed up his pillow, turned out his bedside lamp, and gone to sleep.

Thank God for the book club, she thought now, as she crossed to the nook and settled onto a cushioned chair. Thank God for Louise and Theresa and Charlie.

Thank God Andrea didn't like to cook. Her imprint was largely missing in the kitchen.

And thanks, Katherine Anne Porter, for your tale of love in the midst of the 1918 pandemic and the final days of World War I.

She turned on her laptop, opened up her hard copy of *Pale Horse, Pale Rider*, and paged through the title story.

Young love, she thought, as she read through some of the passages she had marked. How sweet and pathetic.

How fleeting and how deceptive. How promising and how disappointing.

"How I miss it."

When she realized she had said the words out loud, she looked around, as if to make sure no one had heard her. She was strangely embarrassed.

"Too much alone."

She clapped her hand over her mouth. She didn't talk to herself. She never did that.

Charlie would tease her if he were to know. Dear Charlie. She loved Louise and Theresa like older sisters—one kind, one stern—but she loved Charlie in a special way—because he had rescued her when she was, in a very real sense, drowning, and because he knew something about second wives.

"You're a sensitive species," he had said, that afternoon when she had confided in him. "You're so sure you're playing second fiddle just because you're—second."

They had laughed at that. That was the thing about Charlie. He made her laugh, while Greg ...

She loved Greg. She respected him—his intelligence, his skills as a physician, his levelheaded approach to all things personal and professional. If only ...

It sounded so self-indulgent, but she didn't *feel* much anymore. Except for—early in the year, before the general shutdown—that furtive, happy/sad afternoon meeting with Charlie at a local coffee shop. Even in their most intimate moments, Greg seemed to restrain himself, as if too much emotion were unseemly.

She was, she realized, a little afraid of her husband. She adored him, and feared him, in almost equal measure. Why had he chosen her? They met at a dinner party with mutual friends. She thought he was handsome, brilliant, a smooth and entertaining conversationalist. Their courtship was awkward and miraculous. Did he really want *her*, a dozen years his junior, so much her superior in education and accomplishments? She was, at the time, a fundraising associate, tacking credits onto her undergraduate degree year after year without meeting requirements for a master's degree, let alone a doctorate. She had never been able to alight, either in her aspirations or in her love life, until Greg dazzled her.

And now here she was, in her breakfast nook, in the middle of a second Covid-19 surge, working from home with several local charities during the long hours while Greg was at work, awaiting a Zoom call with the three book club friends she depended on to keep her sane and somewhat grounded while the pandemic raged, and her marriage floundered.

"You'll get through this," Charlie had told her, that afternoon at the café, all those months ago. "Greg's a good guy. He loves you. It's just that you and he are living on different planets. You know—*Men Are from Mars, Women Are from Venus.*"

Sybil had laughed.

"You wouldn't remember the book," he said. "It was before your time."

"I'm getting pretty old, Charlie."

"Are you? I thought you were about 29."

"That's because I'm a dunce."

"Don't do that. Don't put yourself down."

He put his hand over hers. They were sitting at a minuscule table, on rickety wrought iron French bistro chairs, their knees almost touching.

"I shouldn't have called you," she said.

"I'm glad you did."

She knew she should slide her hand out from under his, but it felt so good, so comforting.

They talked, for what seemed like minutes but was actually several hours. She told him things about her marriage, about her feelings—things she should not have divulged. Afterwards, she felt guilty, as though she had been unfaithful to Greg. Maybe she had been. More than once, Greg had suggested a therapist. It was wrong of her to make Charlie her therapist, her confessor.

She opened her book again. She needed to clear her mind, to focus.

Tomorrow was Thanksgiving. She and Greg would have dinner together in their outsize dining room, just the two of them, a dinner she had planned to the final forkful. It would be a successful meal; she was a good cook. But they would have little to say to one another. He would compliment her on each dish. She would nod, thank him, go into minute detail concerning the recipe, pray for the dinner to be over so that they could escape, with their pie and coffee, to the TV room, where they would watch a documentary.

She had hosted many successful dinners in that dining room, with Greg leading the conversation in interesting, thoughtful, even exciting directions. But now, with just the two of them, they couldn't seem to get beyond the stilted "How was your day," the polite "Good dinner, hon," and the impersonal "Can't wait for things to get back to normal." She wondered if he were as bored as she was with these endless meals.

As she paged through the book, her eyes alighted on a description of Adam, the young soldier, as seen by newspaper columnist Miranda, his lover—"lover" having a much more innocent connotation in 1918 than it did today. Miranda sees him as "all olive and tan and tawny, hay colored and sand colored from hair to boots."

Like Charlie, she thought—although his hair was going gray. He was only a few years younger than Greg, but he seemed to her so much younger. Her age. Her contemporary. Perhaps because he was so much more—alive.

Miranda goes on to describe Adam as looking, that morning, "like a fine healthy apple."

Sybil laughed out loud at the description. How wonderful to think of your lover as a "fine healthy apple."

Then there's Miranda, as seen by Adam. When she talks about her "unnatural" way of living, with late hours, bad coffee, too much smoking, he says to her, "Why, it hasn't hurt you a bit, I think you're beautiful."

Miranda and Adam would have known each other for ten days when the story begins. She and Charlie have known each other for ten years.

"I'm way too focused on the love story," Sybil said, out loud. "Theresa would scold me."

She smiled, shook her head, continued paging through the story.

Miranda is about to succumb to the "plague" surrounding them. She "winked in the sunlight, her head swimming slowly."

Sybil tried to focus on Miranda's symptoms, underlining the passages, so reminiscent of all she had read and heard about the coronavirus, which Miranda says she can't smell or see. "I must have a fearful cold."

But then she came across the passage about Adam holding Miranda's hands. He pulls at the fingers of her gloves, turning her hands "as if they were something new and curious and of great value." Miranda turns "shy and quiet."

She thought about Charlie putting his hand over hers at the café, pressing down hard, and how she felt at that moment. Yes. Shy. Quiet. Warm. Comforted.

⌒

Sybil continued to page through her hard copy of *Pale Horse, Pale Rider*, in preparation for the book club meeting, which would begin in a few minutes.

She paused at a passage in which Miranda is talking with her newspaper colleagues about the plague. One colleague remarks that "they say" it's caused by germs brought by a German ship to Boston. "Isn't that ridiculous?" the colleague concludes.

About as ridiculous as Trump calling Covid-19 "the China virus," thought Sybil, while he was refusing absolutely to take any blame for his negligence. She marked the passage.

"Theresa will like discussing that one," she said out loud.

She checked the time on her laptop. It was still early. Theresa wouldn't be coming online for a while, and Louise and Charlie usually slid in at the last moment.

She looked forward to their meetings more than she would acknowledge—even to herself. The book club was her reality check during the pandemic, her support team during a tense election period. These were friends who thought—as she did—that masks and isolating were moral imperatives; that the election of Joe Biden nearly three weeks ago would, in a very real sense, save the planet. Rescue the country from tyranny. Salvage the fabric of their lives. She discussed these issues with Greg, and with her friends and work associates, but those three faces on the Zoom screen were her soulmates, ten years in the making, and Charlie—well, he was even more special, now that he had put his hand over hers and comforted her when she needed it most.

She stopped at another passage—a description of Adam, as seen by Miranda, as she enters a restaurant to meet him. She sees him before he sees her—just as Sybil had seen Charlie before he looked up and saw her. Miranda finds her lover's face "extraordinary," "smooth and fine and golden," but melancholy. She pictures him, then, when he would have been an older man, a man "he would not live to be." He greets her, they drink hot tea, and dance. Miranda thinks the music is gay, and "life is completely crazy anyway," so it doesn't matter. "This is what we have," she thinks to herself, "this is all we're going to get, this is the way it is with us."

Sybil read the passage again. They had fourteen days in 1918, she thought, in the middle of a pandemic, in the last days of a world war. I suppose I should be grateful that Charlie and I had three hours, in a neighborhood café, before the pandemic made anything beyond that impossible.

She had come close to weeping while Charlie had his hand over hers in the café. She wanted to weep and rage, but it would draw attention to them, and she wanted this time with Charlie. She didn't want it to end because strangers were staring at them.

Paging through her book, Sybil stops at the passage in which Miranda, in a state of near-delirium, invites Adam to sing with her an old spiritual.

"Pale horse, pale rider, done taken my lover away ..."

She reads on. Miranda is taken to the hospital where, in a prolonged period of near-death dreams and hysteria, she hears bells screaming, horns and whistles, explosions of sound. Her nurse explains that it's the Armistice. "The war is over," she tells Miranda.

"November 11, 1918," murmured Sybil. Miranda's long, drawn-out crisis is nearing its end. She will survive—but her lover will not.

⌒

"I can't go on like this," Sybil had said to Charlie, as they sat on the rickety chairs, knee-to-knee, in the café. She wasn't sick; she wasn't on the brink of death, as was Miranda, but she felt as if her life were over—a puerile, useless thing.

Charlie didn't ask her why she had called him, why she had suggested they meet for coffee, why she was confiding in him. He had agreed, without question, without hesitation, saying very little as she talked, not the Charlie of the book club but a mostly silent, wholly sympathetic listener.

"I know I should be grateful for all I've got, but instead I'm angry, as if I've been denied something that is my right, as if my being relatively comfortable is a punishment for thinking I could make a difference, could accomplish something that would make people's lives better ..."

She stopped, knowing she couldn't adequately express her frustration, but Charlie nodded, said, "I know, I know," over and over, as though those two mundane words were magical—and they were. She talked until she was empty— of words, of anger, of frustration. She felt soothed. She had made the right call. She was sure Charlie was someone to whom she could say the things she was saying.

She couldn't divorce Greg. She couldn't even separate from him. She hadn't the courage, or the resources. She still loved him, and he loved her, in his way. He gave her everything he thought she wanted, but she wanted warmth, attention, affection. His thermostat was always set at 70 degrees, and she was comfortable at 80 degrees or more. Maybe that was why Andrea had left him for another man. Maybe Andrea's thermostat had been set higher as well.

She had tried to retain her job as a fundraiser after their marriage, but taking a salary seemed selfish and pointless, now that she was well off. She still wanted to change the world, to raise money for hospitals and welfare organizations, so she turned to charity work, organizing fundraising events, sourcing funds for the homeless, for kids in poor neighborhoods, helping with Covid-19 projects.

"But I'm still mostly removed from the dirty underside of ordinary life," she told Charlie. "I'll never change anything, make anything better."

"Seems to me you've been doing that all along," Charlie said, cheerfully saluting her with his coffee mug. "Most of us don't give a damn about the so-called 'underside' of life."

In this way, as the minutes turned into an hour, then two, then three, Charlie listened, responded, echoed her concerns. He didn't give her advice or question what she told him, not even with a raised eyebrow. He was just—there for her.

"All I've ever done is raise money—that's what I do, and I've never cared about it, about money, I mean." Charlie nodded his head. He didn't seem bored, or impatient, or distracted, like …

Coming back to the present moment, glancing again at the time, Sybil continued reviewing the pages of her book.

"If only Greg were—there for me," she said aloud. "He's there for his patients, but not for me."

This time, she didn't look around. Talking to herself was beginning to feel natural.

She came across a passage in which Miranda is looking around "with the covertly hostile eyes of an alien." She doesn't like the country in which she finds herself, doesn't understand the language "nor wish to learn it," does intend to live there but is "helpless" and unable to leave at will.

"I'm that alien," Sybil said, loudly, as if to announce it to herself.

She shifted on her cushioned seat, no longer embarrassed by her voice.

"Charlie would approve," she said. "He would listen to this passage and nod his head. Maybe I'll read it during our meeting."

She underlined the words with her darkest pencil and read on. As Miranda recuperates in the hospital, she's given a bundle of letters, but she shrinks from them, unable to make them out. One of them is a thin letter in an unfamiliar handwriting, dated more than a month before. The letter is from someone she doesn't know, someone from the camp where Adam had been stationed, telling her that Adam was dead, that he had died of influenza in the camp hospital. Adam had asked him, "in case anything happened," to let Miranda know.

Oh, Miranda, thought Sybil.

As Miranda gets ready to leave the hospital and take a "taxicab" to her old rooming house, she muses that there will be no more war, no more plague, only "the dead cold light of tomorrow." She concludes, "Now there would be time for everything."

Sybil wept. She had wanted to weep when she sat across from Charlie all those months ago, but she had held herself in. Now, there was no reason to hold herself in. She was alone. She had only to dry her eyes before she met with Louise and Theresa—and Charlie.

So far, the four of them had survived this year of plague and presidential conflict. The plague still raged but the election was a win. Charlie, her keeper of secrets, her hand-holding knight, had put her concerns about Greg in check. At least for now, her thermostat was set at 80 degrees.

She tapped the meeting link, entered her username, and waited for an invitation to join the book club.

November 28, 2020

United States COVID-19 Statistics
Cases: 13,233,022
Deaths: 266,009

December 3, 2020

United States COVID-19 Statistics
Cases: 13,975,104
Deaths: 274,121

Between Friday, November 20, and Tuesday, November 24, five million Americans went somewhere other than their homes for Thanksgiving—pushing up against each other at airport screenings and on the planes, sucking up each other's air, wearing masks (hopefully) voluntarily or reluctantly—having convinced themselves that they were safe, and that their friends and families—up ahead and back home—were safe.

We'll all feel the results of those decisions as time, and Covid-19, moves relentlessly on. The Thanksgiving week numbers—new cases, new deaths—won't be known for a week or two.

The end results of the election:

2020 Presidential General Election
Source: uselectionatlas.org

Electoral Vote
Joseph R. Biden, Jr.   306   56.9%
Donald J. Trump   232   43.1%

Popular Vote
Joseph R. Biden, Jr.   80,960,039   51.24%
Donald J. Trump   74,048,704   46.87%

⌒

The son of a bitch lost. Someone in his family, his cabinet, his legal team, his PAC, should let him know. Bill Barr should let him know. Mitch McConnell should let him know. Rudy Giuliani should let him know. Melania or one of his two ex-wives should let him know. Don Jr., Eric, Ivanka, Tiffany, or his teenage son, Barron, should let him know. Jared, his scoundrel of a son-in-law, should let him know. Someone in his craven cult of yes-men and yes-women should let him know he lost the election. Come January 20, he'll either exit with some modicum of dignity or, obstinate to the end, be escorted out of the White House.

I heard on the news yesterday that Trump has 88 million Twitter followers. Now, if most of those followers had put in their vote for him, he would have won the election handily. However, many of them are tuning in for entertainment value only—kinda like watching "The Apprentice"—just to see people humiliating and being humiliated by each other. Trump made his bones on that show.

Donald Trump—no longer "Sir"—you lost. Get used to it.

December 6, 2020

The pandemic is now killing almost 3,000 Americans every day.

Meanwhile, Trump continues to rage about the election, denying the reality of his defeat. He condemns Republicans who acknowledge Biden's victory as "RINOS" (Republicans in Name Only).

2:30 p.m.

According to a tweet by Trump just now, his attorney, Rudy Giuliani, has tested positive for Covid-19.

Giuliani is the 53rd person in Trump's White House inner circle to contract the virus in recent months. The "super-spreader event" was the celebration of Amy Coney Barrett's nomination to the Supreme Court, which took place in the Rose Garden on Saturday, September 26. It's unclear to me which will prove to be the more destructive to Americans this month and next—the raging pandemic or the raging president.

December 10, 2020

More than 3,000 Americans dead in one day

More than 9/11. More than Pearl Harbor. In a single day. In the year 2020. In the United States of America. More than 3,000 people are dead today that were alive yesterday. How do we absorb the number? How can we shrug and go on with our day?

We have a vaccine coming, okay, but today, right now, there is no vaccine. There are people getting sick and dying of Covid-19. Every day. In the thousands.

December 12, 2020

The cavalry is coming.

The Pfizer Cavalry is trucking across the country via UPS and Fedex even now, with the vaccine the nation has been awaiting for many long months. I've been immured, as have many in this nation, for nine months almost to the day. I began sheltering in place on Friday, the 13th of March. For those of us who have adhered to science and scientists, the wait has been long—and is not over. It will take months to vaccinate 300 million people. We'll start, if all goes well, with the healthcare workers, go on from there to those in nursing homes and other confined spaces (including prisons, I would hope), and then make our way down through the population from old to young.

Meantime, the pandemic continues to rage—and following close behind is our soon-to-be-unseated president, also raging, as he has his lackeys and followers support him in his baseless claims that the election he lost was—because he lost—not valid. Yesterday, the Supreme Court turned down his claims, with 126 House Republicans and 13 state attorneys general among the followers supporting his lawsuit.

His lawyers, however, including the indefatigable Rudy Giuliani, continue to storm the legal citadels. Why, you ask?

How about the fact that Trump has a bottomless piggy bank in the form of donations from a base of 75 million Americans who support and believe in him unquestionably? He has already filled that piggy bank with something in excess of 200 million dollars—and it just keeps growing. Why would he stop? It's passive income of the purest gold.

December 14, 2020

Full disclosure: I've been getting most of my news information from two sources—MSNBC and *The New York Times*. I have many online sources, and other apps on my iPhone—PBS, NPR, NBC, Apple News, *The Los Angeles Times*, *The Washington Post*—but my go-to sources are the *NYT* and MSNBC. I trust the coverage. I like the anchors, the reporters, and the opinions professed. I can read the *NYT* and watch or listen to MSNBC on my iPhone. Truth be told, I rarely turn on the television set for news. It has to be a big event; otherwise, the three-by-five-inch screen on my iPhone is plenty big enough—and often unnecessary, as I am primarily listening to rather than watching the news.

I haven't gotten a real handle on statistical sources for MSNBC or the *NYT* (I think it's primarily Johns Hopkins), but I noted, yesterday and today, the uptick from 298,856 deaths from Covid yesterday at 1:00 p.m., to 300,028, the number announced at 10:45 this morning on MSNBC.

At the very same time, the headline news was that the first Pfizer vaccines were being injected in the arms of critical care workers in selected states throughout the country.

I have to acknowledge both the tragedy and the irony of those two coinciding events.

December 18, 2020

Here's how I feel today.

I feel grateful. I'm still relatively healthy. My family and close friends are healthy. The pandemic rages on, but the vaccine has arrived. Hopefully, the vaccine will expeditiously make its way into many arms.

I feel lonely. More than nine months with almost no social interaction. We are a very social species. Gatherings are important to us. It's unnatural not to get together for such an extended period of time. I miss my family most of all. We're communicating but, quite literally, not in touch.

I feel lighter. I've lost 20 lbs. during my enforced isolation. Because I'm not grocery in-store shopping, I'm much more careful about what I buy. I've made a conscious decision not to buy snacks and sweets. It's hard, but doable. Temptation is in the outside world and I'm, for the most part, inside.

I feel creative. I've continued writing, most days, on this multi-genre work that combines chronicle, fiction, and personal reflection. I don't know what it is, exactly, but it's growing, and I'm looking forward to seeing how it turns out.

I feel frustrated. Not enough money. Too many expenses. Every month is a challenge. Between my disappearing cash and my dwindling credit, will I get through it?

I feel claustrophobic. Too much of my own company. Thankfully, I have a dog. Indi keeps me sane, reminds me when it's time to eat, time to go outside, time to play, time to relax and cuddle, time to go to bed. I can watch her race joyfully around our small yard, but even walking her up and down the street is risky as only about one out of every two or three of my neighbors is wearing a mask.

I feel fortunate. So much sickness. So much death. I've been spared. My family has been spared. We've taken all the precautions, but there's still a generous dose of good fortune that has gone into this year.

December 19, 2020

At 11:15 a.m. I got a text message from my nephew that he had tested positive for Covid-19. He was tested on Monday and has been sheltering at home since then. He is the first person among my family and close friends to test positive.

I called him immediately and we talked for some time. He has a slight fever (99 degrees); he's tired and congested. He described it as "like a mild flu." He said he felt "miserable, congested, run down."

Apparently, he began to feel symptoms last weekend, and got tested on Monday at a clinic assigned by his workplace. He was tested in his car, in the parking lot, and got the results in 15 minutes. He has been quarantined for 10 days.

He had been at my sister's house last weekend, so she was tested, as were other family members who were visitors over the weekend. They have all tested negative.

There is a different vibe when the virus hits close to home, an altered state of mind. It makes it more real, somehow, than all of the statistics and all of the news stories. It has infected someone I know and love. It has endangered others I love. It is all too close—even though those loved ones are far away, in Ohio. It is like a home invasion; those people belong to me, and I to them. I cannot dismiss this, or turn away from it. I cling to the hope that it is mild in its manifestation, that it courses through the body like a flu, and the body recovers quickly, totally.

My only advice to my nephew was that he sleep, that he allow himself to lie idly on the couch and watch TV, that he get out of the way of his body as it recuperates, that he stay away from his workplace for the rest of the year. There's no doubt in my mind it came from his workplace. The longer he stays away the better.

December 20, 2020

If any of us thought we would be rid of Trump when we voted him out, we were incredibly optimistic and/or naive. The pollution of his administration will be poisoning us for many years to come. If we're clear-eyed about the damage he has done, it's endemic, and it's permanent.

He's leaving us, for instance, with a cyber hack of unprecedented enormity. We don't even know how much harm it has already done, or will be doing. He has ignored the evidence pointing directly at Russia and has, instead, nominated his favorite target—China—when the best analysis is that it's the work of the SVR—the Russian version of our CIA.

Is this what it means to be a sociopath? When asked about the damage he might be doing to his legacy, he said he didn't care about his legacy; he would be dead. By any standards—moral, ethical, legal, political, psychological—he exists in some sort of an impenetrable construct, unaffected by ordinary human response.

Trump has checked out as far as this administration is concerned. No response to the pandemic. No response to the vaccine. No response to the cyber hack except for his tweet attributing it to China. No news briefs. No interest in the job except for his continuing assertion that the election was corrupt because he did not win it.

As I heard on MSNBC this morning, this is, and has been from the beginning, "a pretend president who is no longer pretending."

December 21, 2020

How is it possible to miss someone so much?

Theresa sat on the sofa in her living room, Swiffer duster in hand, taking a break from her weekly cleaning and annual Christmas decorating. She had vacuumed the floor. She had dusted the mantel and its framed family photos. She had swept clean the ornate side tables, the pleated lampshades, the chair legs, the intricate frame of her French provincial sofa, which she prized for its design rather than for its comfort.

A small artificial tree stood in the corner, carefully decorated and lighted, with unopened gifts beneath from her children and grandchildren. The gifts were impeccably organized according to instructions on the tags ...

Open this first, Mom! Love, Jill

Come visit in the spring, Ma, when we're all disinfected. From: Leonard, Kay & the Kids

Mom: Save this for last!

This is just a stocking stuffer, Ma!

With love from your favorite (and only) daughter. Haha! Hoho!

There were small gifts from the grandchildren, wrapped with small hands, addressed to "Gramma" and decorated with colorful elementary art.

Her cats, Tony and Cleo, were playing with stray lengths of ribbon. One gray, one black, the cats were siblings—regal, green-eyed, inseparable.

She was ready for Christmas—her third Christmas without Turk.

She missed her children, but Leonard and Jill were middle-aged adults, living thousands of miles away, in Chicago and Boston, immersed in their own matters. She was used to their absence. She was used to being a long-distance grandmother. It was Turk's absence that was like a rusty saw grating against her heart.

He had died quickly, with finality, of a heart attack, a few weeks before Christmas. There was no preparation. He did not have a long history of precarious health, daily meds, quarterly checkups, warnings about changing his lifestyle and habits. He had always been a big man, robust, with an aura of strength and health that turned out to be all too misleading. He smoked, moderately and unapologetically. He ate what he liked, preferably red meat and potatoes. He liked to fish and went on many fishing trips with his pals. He played a decent game of golf. He worked hard—making his way up to district manager for a hardware chain, after working his way through college. He was all man, and all hers—and then she lost him.

When the children were knee-high, they had purchased a house on a steeply inclined street in Echo Park. The house had multiple levels, like the street. The children loved it, and Theresa got used to it. The house was full of steps and surprises, unexpected twists and turns. They filled it with period furniture, books, friends, neighborhood children. It was noisy, teeming with life, suffused with music, classical to popular—sometimes at the same time—doors slamming, shouts and whispers emanating from behind closed doors, feet stomping up and down stairs.

She could manage the Christmas decorations, exchange gifts with her children and grandchildren, appear cheerful when they talked during their FaceTime chats. But she couldn't play holiday music—couldn't listen to music at all during the long winter months—without calling up emotions and pain that had no mitigating feelings of nostalgia. She knew she should filter the holidays through her children, and especially her grandchildren, but she resisted even the attempt to sub-merge her life in theirs. She and Turk had had a life together that was apart from that of their children. She refused to give up the vestiges of that life—not yet, maybe not ever.

She still talked to Turk. It was the hardest of all habits to break. It was how they had shared their workdays, and their time away from each other. Her day as a teacher only came to life when she recounted it to Turk. It became a day-by-day chronicle of the rewards, frustrations, and grinding labor of her profession. He, in turn, would give her brief insights into his corporate workday, leaning against the sink, sipping a beer while she prepared dinner.

"Tessy, I'll wager about ninety percent of my time is spent at meetings, and then meetings about meetings, and then doing follow-up meetings for those meetings. But I don't mind so much. We get into some good fights, and I like a good fight. It livens up the group—and it jolts us into a little forward movement. Then we break for coffee or lunch, or go home. It's not all that bad."

"You're putting me on, Turk," she would reply, giving him a brisk kiss as she worked at the sink or at the counter. *"I know how hard you work."*

"Just for that, I'm going to help you correct papers tonight."

"I'll just have to correct your corrections," Theresa would shoot back. *"Stick to doing the dishes."*

After she retired, he vowed he would follow suit.

"We'll take a cruise, Tessy. How about Alaska? Or maybe Hawaii? We'll see the world in comfort, in a cabin with a deck and a view, on a gigantic ship loaded with good things to eat and drink."

But he had put it off, and then it was too late.

His name was Leonard, but he had been called "Turk" as far back as he could remember. He had distilled the story into a few sentences.

"*My folks said I chased a turkey around the back yard when I was a toddler. I was fearless, they told me. Turkeys can be mean sonsabitches. They called me 'Turk' after that, and it stuck.*"

"Merry Christmas, Leonard, my Turk," Theresa murmured, standing up, walking around the perimeter of the living room as she applied her Swiffer duster to as-yet-untouched surfaces. "Tell me honestly—what do you think about the decorations this year? Too much or too little? We never seemed to agree on that."

"I've been thinking about death," Sybil said, later that day, at their last book club meeting of the year. Charlie had opted out of the meeting. Sybil, Louise, and Theresa were finishing up their discussion of *Pale Horse, Pale Rider*. "We're so saturated with death statistics, it's hard not to think about it."

"Greg must be struggling with it," said Louise, her voice low, sympathetic. "It must be tough, as a doctor, to deal with it every day."

"Yes. He doesn't like to bring it home, but it's there, in the very air we breathe together."

"How does he cope with it?"

"I don't think he does," Sybil replied. "He more or less puts it aside, to contemplate later, when he has more time, more emotional energy."

"He's not able to—talk about it, at all?"

"I've given up trying to open that door," said Sybil. "We talk about—other things, pleasant things, things that don't make him angry and leave me—drained."

"I couldn't talk about Turk for the longest time."

The others waited for Theresa to continue. She rarely mentioned Turk. He hadn't been struck down by the pandemic, but they knew that, for her, his death was still raw, and comparatively recent.

"I liked to look at him when he wasn't looking at me, and not aware that I was looking at him. Remember that passage from the book, the one where Miranda is meeting with Adam at a restaurant, and she sees him before he notices her?"

Sybil shivered, thinking of how, for her, that very same passage triggered the memory of her furtive meeting with Charlie early in the year.

"Strangely enough," Theresa continued, speaking slowly, with effort, "that's how I remember Turk—the way he looked when I caught him off-guard. I loved him then more than any other time—I suppose because he wasn't hiding behind a—joke—or a smile."

"I like that scene, all of it," Louise said, quickly taking up the slack as Theresa stopped, abruptly. "It gives us a sense of the fatalism of both Miranda and Adam. It reminds us that we have only the moment."

There was an unusual silence from the group. They heard each other's murmurs of assent from their rectangular frames, but no one spoke up. It seemed a solemn moment, the conclusion of a year in which they had stayed together as a group while observing the norms of an abnormal time—a time of plague, death, loss, endurance.

Finally, summoning her reserves as a former teacher and a woman of conviction, Theresa spoke up again. Her voice was shaky, but the others felt her determination to have the last word in this, their final meeting of the year.

"Okay, this is my fault. I recommended this book. I wanted us to review the lessons of 1918—the lessons of history. I've wanted, since we read *A Journal of the Plague Year*, to bring the story of a plague year from 1665 into the twentieth century. *The Bluest Eye* got me closer to understanding Black Lives Matter. And now *Pale Horse, Pale Rider* confronts a pandemic that happened, in our country and in the world, only a little outside our lifetimes. It helps me to see, in the context of the story, what death can do to our lives—what it has already done to us."

Theresa visibly gulped, took a deep breath.

"I want to say—I'm trying to say—I appreciate you. You helped me get through another year, a really difficult year, without Turk."

No one spoke up. After a pause, Theresa continued.

"This has been a year notable, above all, for the number of people who have died from Covid-19. I'm trying, as I ride out the year, as I ride out another Christmas without Turk, not to lay blame but to sincerely mourn the loss of those lives. Each death had behind it a story—a life that was not lived out to its natural conclusion. When I think of the story of Miranda and Adam, I think about loss, but I also think about love. I had a love story. Each of us has a love story. I'm trying to hold onto that.

"The last sentence of *Pale Horse, Pale Rider*, is 'Now there would be time for everything.' It's ironic, of course, but isn't it also hopeful? I suppose we could have a meeting to discuss that sentence alone. Having 'time for everything' is not always a good thing. I can attest to that. But it's what we have."

December 29, 2020

The death toll in January could be as high as 400,000. Right now, the death numbers are climbing steadily toward 337,000. President-Elect Joe Biden today affirmed the number might reach 400,000 by the end of next month, as he predicted some months ago. He is not softening the blow. He is saying it as it is. I hope he's wrong. I'm sure he does too. But the numbers keep climbing up and up.

I'm sure I'm not alone in finding myself turning away from these statistics. Earlier in the year, I made regular notes. These days, I see the numbers and my eyes glaze over, my brain checks out. The numbers are staggering, and Los Angeles County is leading the way in terms of infection, and death. I don't go out the front door without a mask—even the few feet to my car or my trash bin. Neighbors regularly stroll down the street maskless, children or dogs in tow, seemingly unaware that there's a deathly plague in the air, often intent on their mobile phones—as if life were somewhere inside the device, rather than in the infected air surrounding them, and in the small humans and four-legged animals in their charge.

We've only vaccinated a little over two million Americans since the vaccine became available, although Mike Pence and others in the Republican Party promised twenty million people would be vaccinated by the end of the year. Not a chance.

Shame on you, Mike Pence and company, for making promises you cannot keep.

Meanwhile, Americans celebrate the holidays by gathering together, crowding our airports, and carrying out their vacation travel plans.

And the lame-duck president—having lost 59 voter-fraud court cases up to and including the Supreme Court—plays golf.

January 1, 2021

The time is just past 9:00 a.m. The day is Friday. The month is January. The year is 2021.

I am stepping lightly into the new year, quietly, reverently, acknowledging my good fortune in being here at all, in not having lost a loved one in the previous year. So many are not here to welcome in the year 2021, so much death immediately behind us, so much more to come.

I've been blessed. I and my imperfect heart have managed to survive and remain relatively healthy through the year 2020, mostly in isolation and solitude, but with the reassurance that family and friends were staying relatively healthy in their separate orbits. I'm prepared to continue my solitary journey into this new year, while the miracle vaccine is being manufactured and distributed among us.

Los Angeles County has been hard hit. More than 10,000 deaths, hospitals overburdened and understaffed. Morgues overflowing. Funeral homes turning away families grieving the loss of a family member.

⌒

Last night, New Year's Eve, 291 deaths were reported in Los Angeles County. Some patients turned away from local hospitals were put in a gift shop, among other makeshift facilities. I suppose lying sick in a gift shop, surrounded by teddy bears and balloons, is better than being turned away altogether.

LA County Confirmed Cases:	771,519
LA County Deaths:	10,359
California Cases:	2,245,379
California Deaths:	25,386

⌒

In mid-December, a 69-year-old man flying from Orlando to Los Angeles collapsed and died during the flight. The cause of death was "acute respiratory failure, Covid-19." As of last Sunday, December 27, 1.3 million people boarded planes for holiday air travel. How many of them were sick when they got on board? How many were seemingly healthy but capable of spreading the virus? How many were exposed, carrying the infection home to their confined (or unconfined) circles? When and how will the spread reach its zenith and begin its descent? Will the people in this country continue to ignore the danger and deny the obvious until they themselves become victims?

⌒

Global Confirmed Cases: 83,718,625
Global Deaths: 1,823,154

U.S. Confirmed Cases: 20,007,149
U.S. Deaths: 346,408

The vaccine has come too late for many people throughout the world; it will have come too late for many people alive and seemingly well on this New Year's Day 2021. Twenty million confirmed cases of Covid-19 in the U.S.: almost a quarter of the world's total cases, almost a fifth of the world's deaths. As any person in this country who has lost a loved one can verify, we have failed the pandemic challenge. We have failed miserably.

January 3, 2021

I began this chronicle with a Toni Morrison quote:

"Like failure, chaos contains information that can lead to knowledge—even wisdom."

I wonder what knowledge, let alone wisdom, we can garner from today's Covid-19 statistics:

Global confirmed cases: 84,959,695
Global deaths: 1,840,878

U.S. confirmed cases: 20,566,479
U.S. deaths: 351,233

⌒

And now, with today's news, a one-hour audiotape of Donald Trump attempting to persuade the Georgia secretary of state, a Republican, to overturn the election results. In a one-hour taped phone call with the secretary of state, Trump insisted that the official "find" the votes Trump needed to win the state—a small matter of some 11,780 votes.

An impeachable offense by a president who has already been impeached.

There's a moment in the audiotape that was, for me, particularly striking. Someone on the call—I believe it might have been Mark Meadows, chief of staff—contradicts, in a low voice, something the president has said, and the president responds, questioningly, in a child-like, pleading voice, reluctant to accept what is being said but acknowledging its force.

The man who continues to hold the office of POTUS for seventeen more days is clearly unhinged, and the virus that he allowed to proliferate is continuing unabated into its twelfth month.

We need some relief from the madness surrounding us. I am running out of the nourishment of hope. The acrid taste and smell of chaos are choking me.

The fatal breath.

January 6, 2021

11:45 a.m. (2:45 p.m. ET). I'm writing this as I watch our Capitol being breached by protesters incited by President Trump. Trump, belatedly, tweeted "Stay peaceful." Too late, Mr. President. The Capitol has been breached; protesters are inside the Capitol building, yards away from the site of this morning's Congressional vote count to validate our incoming president and vice president.

As none of the protesters inside the Capitol have been scanned for weapons, there could be Trump cult members with weapons and/or bombs. There are reports coming in at this moment that some of the protesters have guns drawn as they break windows and storm through the building.

The vice president has been taken away to safety, as have all the members of Congress. There is a protester on the dais of the Chamber floor. The National Guard has been called in.

Someone just said, "We are in a precarious position until we own the inside of the building."

I just heard the number "10,000" as the number of people storming the building.

The FBI and Secret Service may be called in to support the National Guard. It sounds as though tear gas has been used to some extent. Canine units will be called in to secure the building.

Noon (3:00 p.m. ET). A woman has been brought out of the building on a stretcher, "covered in blood," as paramedics attempt to resuscitate her with oxygen.

The president, as of now, has done nothing.

The protesters remain inside the Senate chamber.

Protesters are on the floor of the Senate. I am looking at live television coverage of protesters in the Senate chamber, walking around, looking as though they were after-hours visitors invited to explore the room, which is next door to the vice president's chambers.

12:15 p.m. (3:15 p.m. ET). Word that Nancy Pelosi, Speaker of the House, is safe. She is next in line, after the vice president, for the presidency. Several people have been treated for injuries, and there's a report that one person has been shot.

The vote count has been halted. What happens now?

At this moment, authorities are retaking the Rotunda, followed by retaking the House, followed by—I assume—retaking the outside area of the Capitol.

12:17 p.m. (3:17 p.m. ET). Breaking news that Biden will be addressing the protests at the U.S. Capitol—stepping in where Donald Trump fears to tread.

I'm seeing still photos of protesters lying on the floor, with police standing over them.

A 6:00 p.m. curfew has been issued for Washington D. C.

12:27 p.m. (3:27 p.m. ET). I just saw a live television view of protesters on the Senate floor, with one protester walking from one seat to another taking photographs and/or video of desktop papers with his mobile phone. No police, no security, on site.

12:31 p.m. It's 3:31 ET on Capitol Hill, *now in chaos.*

I'm watching video of a lone security person with a club running up three flights of stairs, trying to stop protesters. He stands at the head of the stairs, club in hand, then runs to get in front of the protesters up another flight of stairs, stops and holds up his club, then runs up again. On the third floor he stands again facing a growing number of protesters and is finally joined by additional guards. They seem to be in a central lobby.

12:37 p.m. (3:37 p.m. ET). The governor of Virginia is sending the National Guard to Washington, D.C. One person has been confirmed shot inside the Capitol. I assume that would be the woman brought out on a stretcher at noon.

12:41 p.m. (3:41 p.m. ET). I just heard the words "police state" uttered by a news anchor.

I'm seeing still photos of a protester dangling outside an upper-story window, security police with guns drawn, protesters hunched behind counters.

12:45 p.m. (3:45 p.m. ET). I'm hearing that this has gone from a "protest" to an "occupation," as a number of people have been injured and one person is in critical condition.

News that President Trump has authorized sending the National Guard to the Capitol. Meanwhile, Capitol Police are requesting help and the Secret Service is responding.

12:51 p.m. (3:51 p.m. ET). Still photo of a protester slumping in a chair—in Nancy Pelosi's office.

Anchor asking, *"Why is there not a larger show of force?"*

Video of police officer, with wire basket, assisting to safety the person hanging outside the Capitol, attempting to take down the American flag and put in its place a Trump flag.

12:54 p.m. (3:54 p.m. ET). Apparently, both the Virginia and Maryland governors are sending the National Guard to the Capitol.

1:06 p.m. (4:06 p.m. ET). Per an anchor: An improvised explosive device has been found inside the Capitol.

1:07 p.m. (4:07 p.m. ET). President-Elect Biden is speaking:

"It's not protest; it's insurrection."

"It's a dark moment."

"I call on this mob to pull back now."

"Certification of electoral vote a sacred ritual."

Quoting Lincoln, he called our democracy, *"the last, best hope on earth."*

He called on Trump to address the mob.

As he walked out of the room after a brief speech, he said, with anger, *"Enough is enough is enough."*

It seemed as though he were directing this remark to Trump himself.

Trump, of course, rallied this morning with these very protesters, then left and hid himself in the White House, while his cult carried out his orders.

1:25 p.m. (4:25 p.m. ET). In a tweet, Trump claimed that the election was "stolen"; told the mob to go home.

By tweet, of course. The very word "tweet" has become disgusting to me.

"American carnage" is the language used by Trump in his inauguration speech. American carnage is what we're seeing today, at this moment, according to Jeh Johnson, former Secretary of Homeland Security.

1:32 p.m. (4:32 p.m. ET). Video of Trump standing just outside the White House, telling the mob to go home, at the same time confirming his conviction that the election was *"stolen"* and *"fraudulent."*

"Go home. We love you. You see how others are treated, who are so bad and so evil." The usual delusionary and contradictory Trump-speak.

1:35 p.m. (4:35 p.m. ET). An anchor suggests Trump may *"pre-pardon"* today's rioters.

1:40 p.m. (4:40 p.m. ET). Reporter saying Congress determined to take up electoral process before the end of the day. Apparently, there is no law saying that they must be on the Congressional floor when they take up the certification process.

1:43 p.m. (4:43 p.m. ET). Senators are considering continuing the vote count from a secure location.

Apparently, fifteen or twenty congressmen were trapped in the Chamber while the mob tried to ram the doors. They were assisted to safety by security police.

1:50 p.m. (4:50 p.m. ET). I'm seeing video footage of National Guard inside the Capitol building. Outside, protesters are being herded down the stairs of the building, with security police lining the upper balcony.

I'm seeing protesters being dispersed, and walking away, but I don't see anyone being arrested. *What's going on?*

It's 4:54 p.m. ET on Capitol Hill, and it's obviously getting darker by the minute. What happens after dark? The outside stairs of the building are still clogged with protesters. Every single person should be arrested. I'm not sure about this, but I think I saw, earlier, a male protester pushing a stroller. I don't know if there was a child inside. The image was gone in a moment.

2:02 p.m. (5:02 p.m. ET). Trump's video is being broadcast at this moment, and from loudspeakers to the protesters. Protester said to reporter, *"This is not the end." "This is what needs to happen." "This will happen again."* Supposedly, on January 20.

I saw a protester meandering past the camera, as the reporter spoke, wearing an American flag.

2:07 p.m. (5:07 p.m. ET). News that flash grenades and tear gas have been seen on Capitol Hill.

Capitol police are physically removing protesters who are seated in the areas where Joe Biden will be sworn in on January 20—the Inauguration platforms. The area is in process of being set up for the swearing-in. There are still crowds of protesters in front of the Capitol, and no police in sight.

2:14 p.m. (5:14 p.m. ET). *"There is no law enforcement to communicate with,"* according to a reporter on site at this moment.

It's 5:15 p.m. ET on Capitol Hill. It's dusk. The Capitol building is lit up. Protesters are being allowed to linger on the grounds and on the steps of the Capitol. *Why are there no arrests? Where are the police?*

I just saw an image of a gray-haired female protester dressed up to look like the Statue of Liberty, holding up a torch, which looks like a paint brush.

It's 5:21 p.m. ET on Capitol Hill. It's now full dark. We're getting aerial views of the Capitol Hill campus and surrounding area.

2:24 p.m. (5:24 p.m. ET). News that the Army is deploying the DC National Guard to the Capitol.

2:50 p.m. (5:50 p.m. ET). News that the woman shot inside the Capitol has died.

News that two incendiary devices have been rendered safe. Washington, D.C., curfew bells ringing for 6:00 p.m. curfew.

3:05 p.m. (6:05 p.m. ET). News that the FBI is investigating the two suspected explosive devices.

3:10 p.m. (6:10 p.m. ET). News that it was VP Pence—not Trump—who deployed the National Guard earlier.

3:14 p.m. (6:14 p.m. ET). News that the House Sergeant at Arms has declared the Capitol building secure. The West Front of the Capitol Building has been taken over by armed forces.

Donald Trump, whose 62 legal challenges have come to naught, had his revenge today.

There has been a call for the president to resign. Per the 25th Amendment, the president is *"manifestly unfit"* to hold office.

3:37 p.m. (6:37 p.m. ET). Speaker of the House Nancy Pelosi has announced that the House will reconvene tonight.

3:42 p.m. (6:42 p.m. ET). *"Dear Colleagues"* letter from Nancy Pelosi (read by anchor Rachel Maddow) re reconvening to confirm Electoral College vote. *"I look forward to seeing you later this evening."*

3:53 p.m. (6:53 p.m. ET). According to the D.C. Mayor's Office, there have been 15 arrests and eight EMS transports.

The Senate is expected to convene at 8:00 p.m.

4:12 p.m. (7:12 p.m. ET). Twitter has locked Trump's accounts, with a warning that the account could be suspended.

That's the first really effective reaction I've heard all day to counteract the insurrection. It is seemingly more than the police, the National Guard, the FBI, etc., have done all day—although I'm hearing—apparently in their defense—that they are being less than forceful "by design."

4:28 p.m. (7:28 p.m. ET). The staff and the press have been allowed back into the Capitol.

At the same time, riot police continue to push back the mob on Capitol Hill.

4:39 p.m. (7:39 p.m. ET). A U.S. attorney from Ohio has vowed to prosecute those from northern Ohio who were involved in the riots.

Apparently, he is one of a number of U.S. attorneys who have vowed to prosecute people who may have traveled from their home state to Washington, D.C., to participate in the insurrection.

4:49 p.m. (7:49 p.m. ET). The House Sergeant at Arms has declared—again—that the Capitol Building is secure.

6:30 p.m. (9:30 p.m. ET). Just heard that Facebook and Instagram, in addition to Twitter, have blocked Donald Trump's accounts.

The Electoral College confirmation was reconvened some time ago.

9:00 p.m. (midnight ET). I'm still glued to the news. I'm watching and listening as commentators come and go, expressing their shock and dismay at the events of this day. I heard that four people died during the riot, including the woman who was shot and three people who died from health-related issues during the crisis. There were 52 arrests. What a pitiful display of incompetence. The Capitol Building was pillaged. Four people died while the rioters were on the premises. Why did it take so long to bring that state of chaos under control?

The Senate continues its confirmation of the state certificates as I write. They have arrived at the state of North Dakota, with 237 electoral votes for Biden and 132 for Trump. They might be interrupted in their smooth progression when they get to the state of Pennsylvania.

I agree with those who think Trump should be removed from office via the 25th Amendment, with the remaining two weeks of his administration in the hands of his VP. I would be astounded if it actually happened.

9:15 p.m. (12:15 a.m. ET). We've arrived at the confirmation of the Pennsylvania vote, with 244 electoral votes for Biden and 157 votes for Trump at this point. The expected objection has been made. The Senate has been dismissed to contemplate this objection—for the next two hours, supposedly. I'm not going to make it to the end of this process.

Domestic terrorism. That's what it's being called.

January 7, 2021

I woke up at 3:40 a.m., turned on live news on my iPhone, and saw, at 3:41 a.m. (6:41 a.m. ET), the Senate wrap up the confirmation of the electoral vote—until yesterday, a mere formality.

Now, we are awaiting the results of yesterday's insurrection. Speaker Nancy Pelosi is calling for the 25th Amendment or immediate impeachment proceedings. Two weeks are fourteen days too many for a dangerous, deranged autocrat to remain in power.

January 8, 2021

3:30 p.m. Breaking news:

"Twitter suspends Trump permanently after inciting mob."

Trump's Twitter account has now been shut down permanently—after Facebook/Instagram led the way. Yesterday's "suspension" lasted only twelve hours, after which Trump was back to his old tricks. Trump without his security blanket. Difficult to envision.

My question: How long before Trump starts up another or multiple social media accounts under thinly veiled pseudonyms? How long before his family members, followers and/or cult members, prepare accounts for him, which will quickly put him back in the social media spotlight?

Trump, and the Trump cult, will survive, and perhaps thrive, despite today's draft of impeachment articles—up for a vote next week—and much talk about the 25th Amendment.

Meantime, how much more damage will Trump do between now and January 20? And what happens at the Inauguration—an event, Trump notified his cult in his last tweet, he will not be attending. He will, in other words, be safely out of the way if further chaos is being planned.

January 10, 2021

I am so weary. I've been in lockdown for the past ten months. I've been an observer of outside events. Even so, I'm exhausted by the cumulative effect of 304 days of stress and unease.

The days since last Wednesday, when the Capitol Building was breached and lives were lost, have been especially stressful. I am aware of the Covid-19 threat from moment to moment, and day to day, especially here in LA County, which is now the center of the U.S. pandemic. Add to that the attempted coup on our legislative center in Washington, the culmination of all the days and months leading up to the election, as well as the suspense as to whether we will make it to the Inauguration without more violence—all of it leaves me struggling for breath, for breathing space.

It all adds up to a lot of strain on my imperfect heart. I hope I make it through this time. I have a lot to write. I have a family who needs my love and generational support. I don't want my life on this earth to end with my being stored in some overloaded refrigerated truck until my body can be put underground.

We are ten days from the Inauguration. Much can happen in those few days. The upside: a possible impeachment, with Trump losing his post-presidential perks and his ability to run for public office in the future. A far less possible upside: VP Pence using the 25th Amendment to walk Trump out of the White House. The least possible upside: Trump, like Nixon, will resign. As I'm hearing on the news that Trump is planning a trip to Texas tomorrow, none of the above is likely to happen.

Psychoanalyst Dr. Lance Dodes called Trump a "delusional psychopath" following the chaos last Wednesday (MSNBC January 8, 7:55 p.m.). While not breaking news, this needs to be said, again and again, by specialists in this and related fields. While Trump has been called a sociopath and given many similar labels, this medical diagnosis hits home for me. He is not fit to hold public office or to incite on social media.

So here I am, talking to myself, hoping for better days ahead, fearful I am too optimistic. No one knows for sure what will happen between now and January 17, when another attack on the Capitol has been threatened. No one knows what will happen on January 20 and beyond. We are a nation under siege, both by the Covid-19 pandemic and an ongoing threat of violence. It is a time of stress for all of us, but I can only reflect my own concerns, here in LA, on a Sunday afternoon, with the coronavirus raging outside my door, and our country in crisis.

January 11, 2021

I haven't yet heard the words, but it's obvious to me and, I'm sure, to many others, that we are in the early days of a civil war. Last Wednesday, January 6, the deadly assault on the Capitol Building was our Fort Sumter.

This is from a website called "Trigger Events of the Civil War":

> *With secession, several federal forts, including Fort Sumter in South Carolina, suddenly became outposts in a foreign land. Abraham Lincoln made the decision to send fresh supplies to the beleaguered garrisons. On April 12, 1861, Confederate warships turned back the supply convoy to Fort Sumter and opened a 34-hour bombardment on the stronghold. The garrison surrendered on April 14. The Civil War was now underway.*

We as a nation are confronted by three simultaneous crises: a raging pandemic, seemingly centered in LA County, where my family and I reside; a president who, unhinged by the results of the election, culminated his days in office by fomenting insurrection; and a far-right cult following that is now out of control and intent on further destruction.

One of the more striking results of this multi-layered chaos is the continuing silence and/or stubbornly consistent behavior of Republican legislators. In hiding with fellow congressional members during the coup, Republicans refused to put on masks while closely confined with Democratic legislators, who (on camera) offered them masks. Others are pushing back concerning the insurrection, defending their position and indicating they will not support impeachment of Trump, which will be voted on in the House in two days. About a third of Republicans, in polls, continue to support Trump. Nothing he does will move them to denounce him. That is becoming increasingly clear, as is the specter of continuing civil war.

<hr />

Impeachment Article 1 charges Trump with "incitement of insurrection." It will be up for vote in the House on Wednesday, January 13—one week to the day from the mob riot at the Capitol Building. The Dems will pass it, but how will the Republicans choose to respond? Their response so far has been disappointing. Senator Ted Cruz has said that he would do what he did again—that is, challenge the Electoral College results—despite the coup.

Anchors and analysts say that, if Trump resigns, Pence could give him a presidential pardon. If Trump does not resign, and chooses to pardon himself, he may find that the pardon does not stick.

Here are some of the appellations I've heard applied to Trump in the past few days—and the past few years:

autocrat, demagogue, authoritarian, dictator, fascist, racist, anti-Semite, Islamophobe, homophobe, xenophobe, misogynist, pathological liar, narcissist—and today, in a *New York Times* opinion column: "a wolf in wolf's clothing." I have a personal preference for the titles that describe his psychological limitations, which are legend.

If the impeachment is confirmed by both House and Senate, Trump will be the first president in history to have been impeached twice. In addition, he will lose his option to run for office again, ever—an outcome that will give me immense satisfaction.

January 13, 2021

Impeachment

9:30 a.m. PT/12:30 p.m. ET

Speaker of the House Nancy Pelosi just opened the two-hour House debate on the impeachment of President Trump. She was followed by Jim Jordan of Ohio, who spoke of the "cancel culture" of the Democrats. The debate is going back and forth, in two-minute segments, from Democratic to Republican speakers. It will last for two hours, then be turned over to the Senate. I'm trying to push ahead with my day, while listening in on the debate on my iPhone. I'm already finding it hard to listen to the Republican arguments.

10:20 a.m.

Rep. Matt Gaetz, Republican, Florida, just referred to "the Biden crime family." He also said, "The Left has incited much more violence than the Right."

1:36 p.m. PT/4:36 p.m. ET

Donald Trump has been impeached by the House for the second time. The vote was:

> Democrats: 222
>
> Republicans: 10

1:45 p.m.

LOL moment: MSNBC anchor Nicolle Wallace just commented to a fellow reporter, "I had to ask myself—did I wear the same thing the last time Trump was impeached?"

January 17, 2021

What happens when an irresistible force meets an immovable object?

The Trump cult of personality is calling us out on this question.

This morning I listened to and read about a new poll from NBC News showing that Donald Trump's approval rating is down just one percent from his approval rating in 2017—to 43 percent of voters nationwide.

In addition, 74 percent of Republicans believe that Joe Biden did not win the 2020 election legitimately, while 21 percent of Republicans believe that Biden did win the election legitimately.

Almost nine out of ten Republicans—87 percent—approve of Trump, compared with 89 percent before the November 3 election.

Trump's approval rating among registered voters remains, essentially, the same as it was before the January 6 insurrection at the Capitol.

Among the Republican voters surveyed, 28 percent said their approval was reinforced by the violence at the Capitol on January 6, while 66 percent said that event did not change their feelings.

January 18, 2021

12:30 p.m.

It's Martin Luther King Jr. Day. We are expected to reach 400,000 Covid-19 deaths in the United States within a matter of hours; we will probably pass 500,000 deaths by the end of February.

These are frightening numbers, tragic, incomprehensible. I sit at my computer, looking out the window at a mild California day, sunny, with friendly shadows from the trees and bushes decorating the sidewalks and street. Occasionally, people walk by. I check to see if they're wearing masks. About half the time, they're not. Nothing seems to impress or move the maskless among us. Everything looks okay, so it must be safe. Or, I won't be dictated to by the government. Or, I'm young; I have a natural immunity. Or, no one else is around, so what's the point?

It is hard for the human mind to wrap itself around a number as large as 400,000—let alone 500,000—while we are still struggling to comprehend the enormity of the 675,000 lives that were lost in the 1918 pandemic.

I have an appointment to get the Covid-19 vaccine at my doctor's office in early March, but I'm looking into getting it sooner, from some local clinic, pharmacy, or makeshift drive-through. I'm hoping I don't add to the swiftly climbing death count in Los Angeles County. I'm doing all I can do to avoid it—mostly by sheltering in place, living alone—my dog, Indi, my only companion—counting the days of confinement, optimistically looking forward to a time of relative freedom.

This is day 312 of my personal lockdown:

March 13–31	19 days
April	30 days
May	31 days
June	30 days
July	31 days
August	31 days
September	30 days
October	31 days
November	30 days
December	31 days
January 1–18	18 days

I'm a writer, I need solitude, I respect its many benefits. But this is so far outside of my experience that I don't know how to deal with it. I'm grateful I've been able to stay safely out of harm's way, but I'm beginning to feel like a nun who has taken a vow of silence, solitude, and withdrawal from the outside world.

None of this matters as I contemplate that, even as I write this, the death toll is climbing relentlessly to 400,000. It may already have happened. I will turn on the news at some point, catch up on arrangements for Joe Biden's Inauguration on Wednesday, listen to news anchors and political analysts reach for additional adjectives to condemn the character and actions of our current commander-in-chief.

His power—at least his state power—ends at high noon ET the day after tomorrow. But the Covid-19 death toll—a death toll that he did little to impede, and cares nothing about now—continues its steady climb. There are no term limits for a pandemic.

January 19, 2021

11:00 a.m.

We passed the 400,000 Covid-19 death toll before dawn today. The soon-to-be-ex-president will carry this badge of dishonor as his legacy, in addition to his "Incitement of Insurrection" impeachment.

After an emotional farewell speech, Joe Biden is about to leave Wilmington, Delaware, for battleground Washington, D.C.

I have been reading, listening to, and watching the news obsessively for months now. I read the news digitally, and I have my iPhone tuned in to news and analysis whenever I'm engaged in activities that don't require my total attention. It's a continual buzz in my head, even late at night, in bed, when I'm having trouble getting to sleep, and in the middle of the night, when I wake up and find it difficult or impossible to get back to sleep. It has become a state of being I now have to modify, before news dominates my emotional life, as it has taken over my attention. Hopefully, the transition tomorrow will give me some measure of calm—as opposed to a constant state of anxiety.

I've noticed that Indi, my little canine companion, has been panting a lot lately. Once she starts panting, it can go on for hours. I'm familiar with her reaction to loud noises, her panting and uncontrollable trembling on New Year's Eve and the 4th of July. I do my best to see her through the hours of fireworks and nearby bullet-like explosions. This, however, is something new. We are such close and constant companions that I wonder if she is responding, in that wondrous way animals have, to my emotional state. She is like my Seeing Eye dog, responding to my moods, echoing my responses, alert to danger, absorbing my anxiety like a 20-lb. terrier sponge. I reassure her whenever she has a panting episode, but I wonder if she is comforted by my "It's okay, everything's okay" mantra—when I'm not sure I myself believe it.

Indi does her best to keep me glued to a healthy daily schedule. In the morning, after she has her run in the yard and her breakfast, she makes sure I'm seated at my computer and firing up the screen before she retires to the bedroom for her nap. In the afternoon, she waits patiently for me to go outside with her, for our "outside time" together. In the evening, after her dinner, she has her last run in the yard and gives me until about 10:00 p.m. to have dinner and relax with a book or a movie. She stays close, relaxing with me, before she stands in the doorway and stares me down. It's time for bed, she says, in no uncertain terms. It's hard to ignore that relentless stare, but I have often done so, defiantly staying up much too late. But I feel best when I respond to her bio-rhythms, and my own—which tell me much the same thing: get up early; get on with your routine; go to bed early; get a good night's rest.

We're still in lockdown. A good working routine is best all around.

3:00 p.m.

I cried—as did, I'm sure, many viewers—while I listened to and watched the brief memorial ceremony at the National Mall a half hour ago. It was 5:30 p.m. ET as the setting sun lit up the Capitol, the Washington Monument, the Lincoln Memorial, the 200,000 flags in the Field of Flags, and the 400 lights—each representing 1,000 lives lost—along the Lincoln Memorial Reflecting Pool.

The words that made me cry were Joe Biden's "To heal, we must remember." It was followed by a few sentences I don't recall. Those five words struck a chord, and that chord reverberated in a way that, for me, was unexpected and emotional.

Biden's speech was preceded by an opening prayer (Washington's Archbishop Gregory), followed by Kamala Harris, who also spoke briefly, and by a nurse from Livonia, Michigan, and a gospel singer (Yolanda Adams), who sang a cappella renditions of "Amazing Grace" and "Hallelujah."

This was followed by about five minutes of silence before they walked away.

I found the near absence of speech very moving.

The National Mall is currently protected by 25,000 National Guard troops. It's on complete lockdown following the January 6 insurrection and preceding tomorrow's Inaugural event.

January 20, 2021

I woke up at 3:00 a.m. It's now 1:30 p.m. In the interim, I've watched the departure of Donald Trump and the Inauguration of Joe Biden.

I wanted to pull myself away from the images of this day-long ritual, but I found it almost impossible to do. It was as if I had to *witness* Donald and Melania Trump's departure—red carpet in place—from the White House to the Marine One helicopter, *watch* as they landed at Joint Andrews Base in Maryland, where a small crowd applauded Trump's last public words as President of the United States, *follow* that familiar black-coated figure as he boarded Air Force One with his wife and family, *exhale* as the plane lifted off and flew away to Florida. I just couldn't take my eyes off the screen until that plane was in the air and getting smaller and smaller ...

After that, I was so enthralled by the ritual and the pomp of the presidential transfer that I continued to watch either my television or my iPhone from hour to hour. Again, I needed to witness the moment when President Biden and the First Lady walked up the stairs and into the front door of the White House—absent the usual ritual of a welcoming former president—and took possession of their new home.

I think I can let go of my news addiction—almost. I think I've seen and heard what I need to see and hear in order to accept that we have, in fact, made the transition. But a part of me still feels like a half-starved child who can't quite digest the food that is now plentiful.

I can watch the rest of today's festivities with one eye and one ear as I begin to get back to—*my* life.

January 21, 2021

The expressions "Reset" and "Radical Normalcy" are not mine, but they are my two favorite expressions of the day. "Reset" to the pre-Trump era. Enjoy again an almost-forgotten concept: normalcy. That's what today feels like to me and to millions of relieved and revitalized Americans, as Joe Biden's administration gets underway. Daily news briefs restarted yesterday, and today Dr. Fauci is again the man of the moment.

I am, for the first time in months, able to get through a workday without one ear and one eye on the news—fearful of what might possibly go wrong during the intervals when I'm not on top of current events. It's the way I've felt, for months, as the election crept closer and my fears mounted. The bogeyman was out there. Would he get to extend his power over us for another four years? It was a horrifying prospect. I, like many, wondered if I felt at home in this country, if there might be somewhere else—maybe Canada?—where my daily life and well-being were not in the hands of a narcissistic sociopath, or perhaps a full-fledged psychopath.

We now seem to be back on track, fighting the battle we should have been engaged in all of last year. Our enemy is a global pandemic, and the U.S. death toll is comparable to World War II. This is our World War III, and now we can focus on putting our troops into battle.

January 22, 2021

"Truth is now just an option."

Those words—spoken this morning on MSNBC by former Senator Tom Daschle—spoke to me. We've opened the emergency exit doors to escape a virtual political and pandemic hell, but the door is still standing open behind us. The fire is still raging inside the theater, and smoke and fumes have escaped, along with those of us who were its potential victims.

Our new president is well-intentioned, sincere, and empathetic. I hope he also has the determination and stamina to persist, in the face of the opposition that is gearing up even now, in the second full day of his administration.

I began to switch gears yesterday, as relief washed over me. My upcoming novel is occupying much of my mind again, as I consider cover art and proof inside pages. I wasn't able to focus on it completely in recent months. I didn't seem to own my own time, my own life, as I witnessed the chaos of the pandemic and the politics of fear and deception. I feel exhilarated, empowered to push forward with all I hope to do in the time that remains for me: visits with family—so near to me but untouchable and distant for nearly a year, novels to write and have published, this very "novel" (for me) attempt to combine nonfiction and fiction in a chronicle of 2020, which I'll continue in the months to come, while we remain in lockdown.

"Like failure, chaos contains information that can lead to knowledge—even wisdom."

Toni Morrison's words continue to guide me. My fervent prayer is that we are all a little wiser for the chaos we have lived through in the past four years.

My own self-imposed lockdown began on Friday, the 13th of March. Today is day 316 of my voluntary sheltering in place. I regret the pandemic that precipitated this long period of isolation, but I don't for a second regret our family decision to safeguard our health and safety.

January 27, 2021

This is day 321 of my personal lockdown (per my January 18 calculation). I'm limping along from day to day—quite literally, as my knees are more or less disagreeable from day to day. Three hundred and twenty-one days—not yet a year but a lot of time has passed and much has happened in the outside world, if not in my own very confined personal and isolated world.

I've never experienced this level of solitude. I wonder how this year would have been without family support, without my writing—without Indi! One needs a dog or a cat in one's solitude. They are the only indoor domestic animals that can intuit our mental and physical well-being. I believe horses, and perhaps some other domesticated animals, have that ability, but most of us cannot stable a horse, so we turn to our canine and feline friends, who fit comfortably into our limited environments.

I have an affinity for terriers and have had three: Indi, Karma, and Casey. I also had a chihuahua way back when. Family dogs have included rescue dogs and numerous sporting breeds: beagles, basset hounds, pointers, English and Irish setters. At one time, we had a cat named Candy. Casey and Candy were good friends. I don't remember any other household cats as I was growing up. Cats came and went freely in our neighborhood. Mostly, they were temporary boarders.

During the past 321 days, and in the decade or so preceding, Indi has become very attuned to me. I have also become quite literate in doggie-speak. We understand each other and depend on one another. She, of course, is totally dependent on me, but I freely admit to being very dependent on her as companion in my solitude.

⌒

Indi-speak

The stare:

    a.   I need to go outside (usually from the vantage point of the kitchen door).

b. It's time to go to bed (infallibly, between 10:00 and 10:15 p.m.).

c. Feed me (when I bypass her infallible internal timer).

The circling:

a. I need to go outside—or do something else equally important.

b. I am anxious about something (especially loud sounds like fireworks).

c. I'm in panic mode (when loud sounds trigger panting/trembling/circling).

The whimper:

a. It's time to get up/pay attention to me! I need to go outside!

b. The halter and leash! We're going for a walk! Yay!

c. It's something yummy to eat! Hurry up! I can't wait!

The bark:

a. There's someone knocking on the door or ringing the bell.

b. There's someone close to the house who shouldn't be there.

c. There's a cat or dog (known or unknown) lingering in the vicinity.

d. I know the mailman, but I still like to bark when he arrives.

The huff:

    a. I give up. You won't play with me/feed me/put me outside/go to bed.

    b. I'm tired of waiting for you to do something/anything except sit at your desk.

    c. I can only be ignored for so long before I get really mad and stalk out of the room.

January 29, 2021

"So far, this has been a hellish month. I didn't think things could get worse than they were last year, but January 6th proved me wrong, and now ..."

With these grim words, Charlie lit up his Zoom frame and greeted the book club members, adding, "Which is why I thought *The Plot Against America* would be a good choice for us."

"I agree," said Sybil. "It's a metaphor for what happened at the Capitol."

She paused, took a moment to examine the backdrops in which she met with her friends online—Theresa's ornate living room furniture, Louise's book-lined studio, Charlie's self-described playroom. It was comforting to see them in their environment, and to remember being guests in their homes before the onset of the pandemic. She knew her friends admired the roomy kitchen visible from her frame, and the comfortable trestle table around which they had gathered many times in past years.

Then she continued.

"The book is amazingly prescient. Philip Roth died a few years ago or he might be considering a sequel."

"It's interesting," said Louise, "that it's a novel but, true to his autobiographical style, he uses his own name and family history. And the plot—anti-Semitic Charles Lindbergh rather than Franklin Roosevelt is elected U.S. President in 1940—takes history in another direction."

She stopped for a moment, then continued.

"Roth said somewhere that, when he writes fiction, he's told it's autobiography, and when he writes autobiography, he's told it's fiction. He said he'd leave it up to the critics to decide but—being Roth—he didn't say it that politely."

The others didn't comment, so Louise went on.

"Today's far-right rhetoric has gone beyond anti-Semitic to new heights of disgusting. Now, thanks to Trump and the so-called election 'hoax,' the far right has gathered together an army of Islamophobes, xenophobes, nationalists, racists—all welcome as long as they conform to the white supremacists who constitute the core—however twisted that 'core' may be."

"Like it or not," said Sybil, "we're in an undeclared civil war. It's truly frightening."

Theresa spoke up.

"The first line of the book is, 'Fear presides over these memories, a perpetual fear.'"

"Kinda like I've been feeling lately," she added, shivering a little.

"Right," said Sybil. "Philip, the narrator, is just a kid, so he sees things from the perspective of his parents, his older brother, Sandy, their friends and neighbors."

"It's really chilling," said Louise. "Roth is remembering 9/11, of course—the book was published in 2004—but what we experienced on the 6th, and what we're still experiencing is, like Roth's book, *domestic* terrorism—the other side of the same coin."

"It's devastating to know we have white supremacists on Capitol Hill, representing our country in Congress," said Sybil.

"God help us," Louise responded.

Sybil smiled, but her tone was somber.

"So, all together, and once more, why are we reading books written over the last three hundred years when we could be reading *The New York Times*?"

Louise and Theresa took a few moments to murmur, to shake their heads. Then Sybil continued.

"For me, it's because books contain the lessons of history—and we must learn from the past if we're not to repeat our blunders endlessly into the future."

"Too late," said Charlie.

"Maybe not," she replied.

"The lessons of history—" Theresa began, in her most pedantic tone.

Charlie spoke up, cutting her off mid-sentence.

"Look, Zoombies," he said, "I can't play this game today. I'm not up to it. We need to have a real discussion or I'm outa here."

"I thought that's what we were having," said Theresa, in her most acidic tone.

"Yeah, well, you call it what you like. I call it academic and evasive."

Sybil spoke up before anyone else could respond.

"Charlie, this is important to all of us—everything that's going on—as well as the impact of books on our lives."

"Film is more relevant than books today—by almost any standard," Charlie shot back. "I'm reminded of that every workday. The question I'm wrestling with—even though I suggested the read—is, how is *this* book relevant?"

"I thought that's what we were talking about," said Louise. "Before you stopped us."

"Sorry, Louise," Charlie said, "but I'd rather leave high-minded discussions for *The New York Times* Opinion column. This book is about Jew haters. How they—in some parallel universe—took over our country—in the same way they actually did take over Germany eighty-some years ago. The way they almost took over the world. What the hell kind of people do we have in this country who can get away with killing, maiming, destroying a national monument, then walking away from the scene of the crime? Meanwhile, Trump sits out his last days in office and then boards Air Force One for Mar-a-Lago, where he plays golf while waiting for the Senate to acquit him. Philip Roth's world wasn't a parallel universe—we're living in it!"

All three women began to speak at once. There were some moments of confusion, then Theresa made herself heard.

"Get off your high horse, Charlie," she said. "You're not the only one angry and brooding over what happened this month. We're all trying to make sense of it—all of us, that is, who condemn what happened, and put the blame squarely where it belongs—on Trump."

"I think we all know we can't solve any of the problems facing us by reading books," said Louise, overriding Theresa's voice. "But isn't the real question how do we live through this? How do we make it bearable? How do we connect when we're stuck in our homes—'Zoombies,' like Charlie says?"

"Charlie," said Sybil, speaking up when Charlie didn't respond. "What is this about, really?"

The others waited as Charlie's frame continued unlit.

Sybil persisted.

"Something has changed, Charlie—something in your life. What is it?"

Louise and Theresa sensed the importance, and the awkwardness, of the moment. They remained silent, knowing that he and Sybil had a special bond.

"Is it—are Joan and the boys okay?"

"Yep," said Charlie, promptly. "They're good."

"Then what—what's going on, Charlie?"

"It's like—" Charlie hesitated, searching for the right words. "It's like when Philip Roth and his family are in Washington, D.C.—sightseeing—and they look up in the air and see the Lindbergh plane flying overhead. It's close and— *ominous*. Not the famous plane that flew across the Atlantic on a solo flight and made Lindbergh a hero, but—now a threat, a warning sign. Then the Roth family is unceremoniously tossed out of their hotel. Why? Because they're Jewish."

"Is that what's going on, Charlie?" Sybil persisted.

"No. Yes. I don't know." Charlie hit his brow with his fist. "It's what's looming in the air over us all. It's what happened at the Capitol on January 6. It's the pandemic. It's open season for hate and violence—people dying—"

Sybil's voice was quiet but insistent.

"Who died, Charlie?"

"You don't know him—"

"It doesn't matter, Charlie. Who was it?"

Charlie clamped down on his teeth, his jaw visibly hardening. His reply was barely audible:

"Nate. Nathan. On the editing team. My boss way back when. Wife called me this morning ..."

He shuddered.

"Happened fast. Hospitalized for a few days. Had all the best care—"

He looked around at the three women, absorbing their almost palpable sympathy.

"Was scheduled for—what do you call it?—monoclonal antibodies."

"Oh, Charlie ..."

Sybil's voice was a moan, a lament they all shared, silently.

"We can stop now—"

"No, goddammit."

Charlie sat back in his office chair, looked out of his window for a few moments, then looked back again at the screen.

"I need this," he said, "this sort of discussion—but it has to be real, it has to be meaningful. We're going to have a half-million dead people missing from our lives in the not-too-distant future. I just want this one life—Nate's life—to *matter*. We worked together for almost twenty years. It was like losing one of you. What's that phrase from *Shadowlands*—'*We read to know we're not alone.*' That's why I read with you lovely ladies. You're an important layer of my life—after my family, one of the most important layers. But let's keep it real and down-to-earth, because what's happening in this country is real and—well—to be honest—it's goddamned terrifying. We're being clobbered by the pandemic, just like we were clobbered by a political system that went completely wacko for four long years. Then the attack on the Capitol happened. And now Nate ..."

He took a deep breath.

"I need to stay on track, stay centered, somehow. I don't know if a book—if *this* book—is gonna do it for me—even though it seemed like a good pick a while back. But I do know what I *don't* want. No feel-good philosophy. No fantasies about the future. Just looking squarely at a country where we *thought* we were safe to bring up our kids and live our lives. Just calling it like it is—a sick and dying world, where good people die and bad people thrive—and we're stuck with it."

February 1, 2021

It has been a while since I've recorded statistics. It's so disheartening to confront the numbers.

> United States Covid-19 Statistics
> Cases: 26,307,963
> Deaths: 443,186

February 7, 2021

I've come to the realization that I cannot keep up. I can't keep up with the news. I can't keep up with my writing. I can't keep up with my daily To Do list. I'm behind in everything— and I have so much to do.

For example, having rejected the cover image provided by my publisher for my upcoming novel, *Only Yesterday*, I would like to suggest an alternative image, so that the pre-publication process can go on. I've spent endless hours looking at stock photos, so that the publisher has some specific direction from me. I've finally come to one conclusion: I want it to be dramatic and yet somewhat enigmatic—like the story itself. I'm looking for foreshadowing, danger, impending death. I'm looking for a blending of light and darkness—which is why I'm looking at sunsets over the Great Lakes. I like the idea of keeping the image close to home, even though few readers will notice or care. I think what one looks for in a book cover is something that draws one in—that calls out for the prospective reader to open the book and read the first line, then turn over the book and see what's on the back cover. I don't yet have reviews, so the back cover will be, at most, my bio and photo. Not a lot to entice the reader, but there it is.

I've had an image in mind since yesterday. It's sunset over one of the Great Lakes, with a silhouette of grasses gone to seed. It has the mood I'm looking for: the day is coming to an end, along with the grass. It's the end of the day, the end of the season, the end of a cycle of life and death.

Meanwhile, the news goes on. Covid-19 goes on—these days with much attention paid to the vaccines. Donald Trump's impeachment trial begins on Tuesday the 9th—with many stories and much speculation leading up to it. I'm reading, listening, and watching closely—as always.

February 9, 2021

Noon: Listening to and occasionally watching the opening statements in the impeachment trial of ex-president—thank God!—Donald Trump. Emotional at the beginning—13-minute video of the January 6 riot. Emotional at the end—listening to Maryland's Rep. Jamie Raskin recount his own experience on that day, having brought along with him to the Capitol his daughter and his son-in-law—while grieving over the recent death of his son. I was moved to tears by his story.

I was also moved by his paraphrasing Abraham Lincoln, saying that Americans will never be destroyed from the outside. If division and destruction come to our country, Raskin said, if we lose our freedoms, it will be because we have destroyed ourselves from within.

This is not an exact quote, but it captures the essence of what Lincoln said in 1838: "*America will never be destroyed from the outside. If we falter and lose our freedoms, it will be because we destroyed ourselves.*" Twenty-three years later, on March 4, Lincoln, our first Republican President, was sworn in—a month before the onset of the Civil War on April 12.

In the brief break that followed the opening statements, Ari Melber, a lawyer and MSNBC anchor, said, "Criminal trials are always about emotion." I have never considered this, but it seems accurate.

2:00 p.m.: The Senate votes on whether the trial is constitutional. The Senate vote is 56 yea; 44 nay. Forty-four of the fifty Republican Senate members are unmoved by all that happened on January 6, and all that was shown and said this afternoon.

As for the client-side of the argument, anchor Brian Williams described it as "meandering and furious." Anchor Ari Melber described it as "bumbling and nonsensical."

As far as I'm concerned, everything is going as expected. The Dems are ardent and emotional; the Republicans are stoic and unmoved. Nothing has changed; nothing will change. Forty-four Senators dwell, easily or uneasily, in the murky Trump swamp. Trump will be acquitted.

⌐

2:50 p.m.: Got a text message—my first regarding my upcoming vaccination, and in response to my registration a while back. Here's the message:

Registration confirmed.

Hello, thank you for recently registering at MyTurn.ca.gov for updates on COVID-19 vaccination in California. You will be notified when it is your turn to schedule an appointment for a vaccine. For the latest information, visit VaccinateAll58.com.

⌐

Today I sent a suggested cover image to my publisher—not the sunset I had chosen, but a stark silhouette of a wintry tree and a cloudy, monochromatic sunset. The change came about because of the artistic sagacity of my son and daughter-in-law, both of whom picked the image from the many I was considering, including the rosy sunset I had chosen. They were right. Tree at sunset is a strong image.

February 10, 2021

The trial, day 2.

Noon: I heard that Senator Josh Hawley is sitting in the balcony of the Senate, feet up, pointedly ignoring the proceedings as he shuffles papers—perhaps, one analyst speculates, working on the manuscript of his upcoming book.

Meantime, the Dems are presenting their case—overwhelming proof that we have a would-be dictator in our midst. Will the proof—video, audio, tweets, extremist histories, timelines, personal experience—the *merchandising* of Trump's "Stand back, Stand by" message to the Proud Boys—move those 44 Senate Republicans, including the impassive Senator Hawley? Not a chance. But there is a vast television audience out there who may be unfamiliar with the ex-president's moral compass. Perhaps a few of those 74 million souls who voted for Trump are rethinking their choice.

February 11, 2021

The trial, day 3.

I've been listening to the trial—working at my desk at the same time—while the prosecution winds up its case. I'm impressed by the arc of their argument—moving inexorably from recounting the event itself to Trump's involvement, to the extremists and their response to the ex-president's call to action, from there to the physical and psychological damage done to the Capitol occupants, both members of Congress and staff—and in particular to the security police trying valiantly to protect the Capitol and those targeted for capture and assassination—in particular, VP Mike Pence and Speaker of the House Nancy Pelosi.

All of this careful preparation won't make a difference in the outcome. Trump will be acquitted, but I wonder if there's any way, legally and with finality and without a Senate conviction, that we can keep him out of office for the rest of his life. That's what I was hoping for at the start of this process, am still hoping will come to pass.

Whew! Take a deep breath.

February 12, 2021

The trial, day 4.

The case for the ex-president was mercifully brief—2 ½ hours of the sixteen hours allotted for the defense. A question-and-answer period followed, limited to five-minute responses. As I listened, I worked at my desk on tasks that did not require my total concentration. There was plenty of room left over, even in my smallish brain, to listen to the rickety defense of Donald Trump—notably an eleven-minute video—with musical soundtrack—of recognizable Congressional Democrats saying the word "Fight" in every conceivable political context. There's a final session tomorrow, after which will come the predictable acquittal.

Trump will get off scot-free, the Republicans will smirk, and the Dems will carry on. There's nothing else to do—except to trust to the courts to sue the bejesus out of him. Seventy-four million voters will feel their vote has been validated. Thousands of rioters will be convinced their attack on the Capitol on January 6 was justified. The legions of extremists hiding in plain sight will make a Josh Hawley fist and continue with their plans to destroy our democracy. And the ex-POTUS who, I've heard, has been playing golf this week, will be free to lead his cult onward and downward.

I heard one of the two Trump lawyers refer to "the framers of the Constitution, such as Woodrow Wilson." But that may have been a momentary lapse, not at all in keeping with their usual aptitude—such as their stirring "Fight" video.

February 13, 2021

The trial, day 5.

As expected, ex-president Trump was acquitted. The Senate vote was 57 guilty; 43 not guilty. Sixty-seven guilty votes were needed for conviction.

Unexpectedly (for me), Mitch McConnell made a long speech following the acquittal, condemning Trump, and almost gleefully noting that the ex-POTUS can be tried in civil court for his many crimes. Even though he's obviously planting his feet firmly on both sides of the fence, I found his belated condemnation very satisfying.

I also heard—and this was of primary importance for my own personal peace of mind—that, by a simple majority, the House can ban Trump from holding political office. This will also entail some sort of court process (which I don't yet understand)—but if the outcome is that he will never again hold political office, I would be relieved. Of course, we would still have to deal with the Trump family—Ivanka, Jared Kushner, Junior, and Eric—but it's a good start.

I want to get back to my *life*. I'm not a journalist and this is not a carefully balanced news summary. I'm writing a chronicle of the plague year that has been dominated by political fireworks. I'm writing a memoir that includes some personal experiences and memories. I'm writing a story about a book club that meets on Zoom and deals with personal issues while hoping to survive a deadly global pandemic. I don't yet know how or when it will end. I hope I'm alive and well enough to finish it and get it out in the world, as I have gotten my four (so far) novels out into the world.

February 14, 2021

The 14th Amendment.

I looked it up and found the words I was looking for:

Constitution of the United States
Fourteenth Amendment
Section 3
No Person shall be a Senator or Representative in
Congress, or elector of President and Vice-President,
or hold any office, civil or military, under the United
States, or under any State, who, having previously taken
an oath, as a member of Congress, or as an officer of
the United States, or as a member of any State legisla-
ture, or as an executive or judicial officer of any State,

to support the Constitution of the United States, shall have engaged in insurrection or rebellion against the same, or given aid or comfort to the enemies thereof. But Congress may by a vote of two-thirds of each House, remove such disability.

Sadly, this amendment, which describes exactly Trump's culpability, and would bar him from holding political office in the future, requires a two-thirds majority of both Houses of Congress, so it's dead-on-arrival. However, the House of Representatives could pass a resolution based on this amendment, put it into the record as an adjunct to the second impeachment, and force the Senate to vote against justice once again.

The day-after analysis of the Republicans and their Senate leader, Mitch McConnell, is inevitable but won't change anything. McConnell made a carefully considered political move, the Republican Senators stuck to their guns, and all is as it was—a world in which Donald Trump is still alive and well and vigorously trampling on our democratic system of government.

Meanwhile, as I've said before—more than once—I'm trying to unleash myself from my now habitual activity of following political news and analysis. I got through the presidential debates, the nomination, the voting season, the resounding Biden/Harris win, the painfully extended attempts by Trump to overturn the election results—leading up to the insurrection on January 6 and its tragic violence and aftermath—and, finally, the second impeachment and trial. All I did was to write about it—and vote. What I did will make no difference in the short run. Most of the words I've written have been seen only by me. I hope it will be of some value in the future, but there are no guarantees. This document may never be published. It may never be available to a larger reading audience.

Nevertheless, I'll keep working on it. Writing has kept me sane, kept me occupied, given meaning to my self-imposed isolation for the past eleven months. This is Day 339 of my lockdown.

My novel *Only Yesterday* will be published soon. It will be good to turn my attention to the cover design and a final proof of the words within.

February 15, 2021

Today, according to covidusa.net, there are 485,943 Covid-19 deaths in the United States, which has a population of 330,756,000.

Worldwide, according to *The New York Times*, there have been more than 2.4 million deaths from Covid-19.

For most of those who died, there is an obituary to be found through a local or regional channel, online and/or in print.

I have become a digital reader during this past year. I love holding a book in my hands, but I am conditioned now to be somewhat fearful of anything arriving from the outside world. I scrupulously wipe down and wash my groceries. I try not to open mail or packages for a day or two. My newspaper subscriptions are digital. I have let my magazine subscriptions lapse. I read books on my iPad; I check out library ebooks from the Los Angeles Public Library via apps like Libby. Obituaries, when I read them, are usually online, unless someone thoughtfully cuts one out of the local newspaper and mails it to me.

An obituary is an interesting document. Someone left behind after the death of a friend or relative sits down and summarizes the life remembered in a few paragraphs. He or she may write this alone or as part of a group effort to memorialize a life that was notable only to a few. Yet, that life may have been more worthy of remembrance than that of a celebrity. But words are hard to find when one is not used to stringing them together, and emotional connection is even harder to define and make concrete. So, a typical obituary will describe a "loving" husband, wife, mother, father; "active" in one or another community organizations; a "devout" member of the local church.

Perhaps we should consider writing our own obituaries —a sort of practice summary of our lives. We could rough it out in our twenties and thirties, fill in personal and career choices in our forties and fifties, summarize our accomplishments in our sixties and seventies. In our eighties, if we're fortunate enough to live that long, we could look back on the evolving structure that has become our obituary. That would be the time, if we've fallen short in any aspect of our lives, to edit and rewrite history. After all, no one has said, no rule has been laid down, that specifies an obituary has to be altogether accurate. By that time in our lives, a little light fantasy might be entertaining—even welcome. Who, one might ask, cares? Those who see through the artifice may recoil in distaste, or smile in appreciation, but it is, after all, an *obituary*—a death notice about someone who is no longer around to praise or chastise.

So, having neglected to draft and build upon this ultimate document of a life in prior decades, I'll just dive in and see what a late-in-the-day synopsis might "look like"—to use a contemporary expression that I hear everywhere these days and one that I particularly dislike.

⌒

Toni Fuhrman died on [month and day] of natural causes. She was a resident of Los Angeles for many years. She is survived by her son and daughter-in-law, two grandsons, her sister, two brothers, seven nieces and nephews, and their children and grandchildren. She was sustained during her lifetime by a loving family and dear friends, including, in later years, LA poet Holly Prado's writing workshop.

Toni grew up in a small Ohio town near Lake Erie, where she graduated from the local high school. She earned her bachelor's degree *cum laude* from the University of Detroit Mercy, where she was a member of the literary honor society, Lambda Iota Tau. She earned her master's degree in English Literature from Case Western Reserve University, and taught composition for Kent State University.

Toni worked in the fund-raising field in Cleveland and Chicago. After moving to Ann Arbor, Michigan, she worked as a creative services consultant and a creative director. She studied writing at the University of Michigan and the University of Windsor (Ontario), taught composition at

Washtenaw Community College, and was certified as an Iyengar Yoga instructor.

She lived in London for six months while writing her first novel, and in Pune, India, for two months while preparing for her yoga certification.

Toni was devoted to her family, and to her writing. She lived in the Midwest for many years before moving to Los Angeles. It was during the LA period of her life that her novels, which she had worked on for many years, were published. The novels include *One Who Loves, The Second Mrs. Price, A Windless Place, Only Yesterday,* and *Everything Earthly.* Other publications include *Imperfect Heart,* a chronicle of the 2020–2021 pandemic and social/political crises; *Liberation and Other Fantasies,* a short story collection; and *What Was I Thinking?,* a collection of essays, most of which were first published on her website.

She will be missed, and remembered, by those who loved her. She "lived faithfully" her chosen life.

February 17, 2021

Today, Donald Trump's Atlantic City casino was demolished. It had been empty for seven years and was considered an eyesore and a safety hazard. I watched it crumble in a huge cloud of smoke and dust a number of times today, on video. It took only a few seconds for it to go from upstanding building to rubble. It seems timely and symbolic—as is the death today of Rush Limbaugh, Trump's precursor and subsequent foot soldier.

February 18, 2021

I was on FaceTime with my younger grandson when NASA's Perseverance rover landed on Mars at 12:55 p.m. It was stunning, and so satisfying, to know that this mission was successfully completed in a time of chaos and pandemic.

～

Meanwhile, back at the ranch ...

Except for El Paso and one or two other border communities, Texas has its own grid system—unlike the rest of the country, which has an Eastern grid and a Western grid. The Lone Star State apparently decided they could do it on their own, avoid government interference, and rake in the profits resulting from their choice of independence.

That is, until a severe winter storm and record low temperatures this past week damaged that infrastructure, disrupted services, including water supplies, caused widespread blackouts, and contaminated supplies for some 12 million Texans.

Sometimes it pays to accept a little government interference.

February 21, 2021

The euphemism "lives lost" is particularly appropriate for the pandemic. These lives were, in a very real way, lost to the spread of a virus that could have been contained, had we harnessed it early last year. But that was not to be because, among other factors more or less beyond our control, we had a brutal autocrat in the White House who refused to confront the facts and the science.

So here we are—those of us who have survived—a year later, confronting a number that exceeds the imagination. A half-million souls—comparable to eradicating any medium-size city in the United States—most of whom made our lives better, richer, more satisfying; surviving now only in our memories, our family histories, our genes.

February 28, 2021

"I'm bowing out for now, ladies," said Charlie.

"Wait—what?"

"You're not serious!"

"What brought this on?"

Charlie nodded as he examined the three familiar faces in their Zoom rectangles. Their responses matched them so well: Sybil's pop-culture expression of surprise and disbelief, Louise's obvious disappointment, Theresa's indignation. Such appealing faces, so engaging in their intelligence, their generosity, their annoying and endearing quirks. But he needed to get away from them, and most everyone else—for now.

"Is it about Nate?" asked Louise, her voice, her expression, sympathetic.

"It is, and it isn't," Charlie replied. "His death hit me pretty hard. He was healthy and normal one day—part of our ongoing editing team—then he was gone—dead—a few days later.

Another Covid fatality. I still can't take it in. He was going strong, in his early sixties …"

"We can meet whenever you like," said Sybil. "Read what you like …"

"It's not about that," Charlie began. Then he stopped.

"Charlie, if it's what you want …"

"Thanks, Louise. I knew you'd understand."

He inhaled, exhaled, as though he had just completed a brief but strenuous sprint. Charlie, who had played quarterback in high school football, sometimes felt as if a couple of heavyweights from the opposing team had collapsed on him.

There was so much he couldn't talk about, even to these obviously sympathetic women. He couldn't talk about Nate's death, not really. It was too painful, too unreal. It was as though it had happened in a book and he didn't want to open that book, or read that page, ever again …

He couldn't talk about Joan, about her impatience with him lately, the brief, dutiful sex, the way she turned away from him, avoiding eye contact, not really listening to him if he talked about his work, or about office politics.

Joan needed him right now, and he wasn't giving her what she needed from him. She was short-tempered with the boys, resentful of anything that distracted him from her or from them, including whatever book he was reading—as if it were a deliberate attempt to get away from her. She changed the subject if he brought up the book club.

Then there was the way the boys were dealing—or not dealing—with online schooling, a year away from their friends and other social contacts—the addictive video games, the temper tantrums, the shouting matches, the tears, the fights with each other, with him, with Joan ...

"It's like this," he said. "I enjoy reading books, and discussing the books I've read. It's like the book doesn't really count unless I've talked about it with somebody. That's why I got together with you guys, what was it—ten years ago? You know all that. But this last year, this last book—and I suggested the read, so this doesn't fall on any of you—it got to me in a way—well, it got to me in a big way.

"Okay, it's what happened to Nate—he was my friend, my mentor—and this goddamned pandemic—and it's the way *The Plot Against America* seems to echo the close call we had with our ex-president. And it's what's being done to suppress the vote. I never heard the word 'fascist' so much in my life as I did in the past few years—until I read this book.

"We've been living through a version of Roth's 'America goes fascist' story eighty years later—and I can't seem to cope, and I don't want to discuss it anymore, or anything else on anyone's reading list. I just don't want to read books for a while. Not until I get a handle on things. Not until I get my head on straight and know where I'm going from here on in."

When there was no immediate response, he added, "Does that make any sense?"

Sybil and Louise both spoke up at the same time. Louise stopped, and Sybil continued.

"Of course it does, Charlie. We're with you on that. Reading it was—I could feel the hair on the back of my neck stand up, I got goose pimply, as I read through it. It's an alternate reality that makes sense in our time ..."

"When I think about it … Charles Lindbergh, famous for something that had nothing to do with politics—a test pilot who flew across the Atlantic—nominated for president and then *winning* it in 1940 … Charles Lindbergh, openly supporting Hitler, more or less openly anti-Semitic, in office in 1941 instead of Roosevelt …

"Then there were those feel-good movements like 'Just Folks' and the 'Good Neighbor Project' breaking up Jewish communities, diminishing their voting strength …"

"We all made those connections, I'm sure," said Louise, picking up the discussion, "and the implications are horrific. But, Charlie, don't let it—don't let this novel—drive you away from us, from our group. We need each other, especially now."

"It's not just the novel," said Charlie, his voice weary.

He leaned back in his chair and surveyed the three faces looking at him. He wondered if he could do it—if he could turn his back on them. On Sybil—that still-young, still-eager face, short dark hair framing her delicate features. Sybil was needy, he understood that, and she needed him more this past year than ever before. And fair Louise—thoughtful and reflective, more mature than Sybil, more insightful.

But there was so much attraction in Sybil's relative naïveté. She made him feel strong—stronger than he felt with Joan lately, more authoritative than he sometimes felt with his own boys …

Then there was Theresa—gray-haired, strong-featured, handsomely imposing. She was the "strict teacher" element in the group, but with a kind heart. She was missing her center—her late husband, Turk—so she used her energy to keep her house in order and her book club friends in line. She was formidable. You didn't mess with Theresa and get away with it.

Charlie looked at the three women looking back at him and felt a sudden compulsion to retract everything he had said, as if Theresa had rapped his knuckles with a ruler in front of the whole class. But he resisted the urge to back down. At fifty, he was the bridge between Sybil and the older women; he helped to make the four of them a cohesive group—but for now the bridge was down.

"I think Roth went a little too far putting up Walter Winchell as a presidential candidate—and then having him assassinated," said Theresa, as though Charlie's decision was no longer under discussion and it was time to get back to the book. "I mean, he was a gossip columnist, for Pete's sake."

"Right," said Sybil, "and Trump was a reality show personality."

"The whole book is off the wall in so many ways," said Louise. "And yet ..."

"And yet," Charlie said, "here we are again. Same old story reel. Democracy in peril, like the damsel-in-distress in silent-movie days—tied to the tracks by the villain, while the train gets closer and closer ..."

"I don't think it will come to that," said Theresa, assuming her pedantic tone. "Not in this day and age."

"Charlie's right," said Sybil. "Philip Roth is right. So far, democracy has survived, but we can't take it for granted. Not anymore. If Trump had been reelected, we might have failed. If January 6 had gone another way ..."

"I don't believe that," said Theresa.

"The Roth family find it impossible to believe," said Louise, quietly taking up the discussion, "until it happens to their neighbors, and then to them. A neighbor and his family escape to Canada, but most of their acquaintances take the optimistic view, until it's too late for them. Until they're 'relocated.' Until they disappear."

"It's a scary book," said Sybil. "It took guts for Roth to write it—to set it in the 1940s, to change the course of history, to put himself in the book, to use his own family, his own family name ..."

Theresa interrupted her.

"But to say that it might happen here, that we might be taken over by the extremists, that we might elect someone who would throw over our democracy ..."

"A few years ago, I would have agreed with you," said Louise. "But now ... How many states are trying to suppress voter rights in this country right now, today?"

"Last I heard, most of them," said Charlie, somberly.

"Right," said Louise. "Republicans are doing everything they can to make sure the kind of voter turnout we had last year doesn't happen next time around."

"But that's out *there*," said Sybil, an edge of desperation in her voice. "That's not us. We need to stick together. Books are what brought us together, but our friendship—"

She stopped, seemed to choke, took a breath.

"Our friendship has kept us together all these years. That—and our love of books."

Charlie shook his head.

"I get what you're saying, Sybil, but it's not gonna happen," he said. "Not now. Not with me. We're friends. That's not gonna change. Not ever. But—"

He coughed, put the back of his hand up to his mouth, as if he were in the room with them, turned his head to glance out the window of his playroom, then looked at the screen again.

"I like reading books. They're solid, real—sometimes more real than what's going on around me. And what's inside them sometimes rocks my world. Books—and the three of you—get me outside myself, outside my tight little community of filmmakers, techs, film buffs, school moms and dads ...

"But I'm a film guy, first and foremost. I'm glued to the industry. You gotta know that about me, after all these years. Books might have helped save the world a hundred years ago, but nowadays they're largely irrelevant. People want images, not words. They want games, not real life. They want to be entertained, not informed. Books are no longer so much an industry as an endangered species."

"That's harsh," said Sybil. "That doesn't sound like you, Charlie."

Even though it was Sybil, Charlie couldn't soften his response. He was trying not to feel—anything—but Sybil's voice, the worry lines between her brows, her dark eyes squinting slightly as she stared at her screen, were troubling.

"It's how I'm feeling these days," Charlie replied. "I can't handle anyone else's problems, even if it's happening in a book. It's all I can do to deal with what's happening in my life, with my family. I'm played out. The isolation, the fear, the frustration, the death. It's so goddamned unrelenting. When do I get to go back to work? I'm sick of this fucking playroom. When does Joan get to stand in front of a class again? When do the boys get to go back to school, to birthday and swim parties, to sleepovers? When do we get to be normal every-day people again? I'll do what I need to do till then—but I'll be focusing on family and work, in that order …"

He knew there was nothing he could say that would jus-tify, to them, his "leave of absence." He knew only that he was temporarily beyond the reach of their friendship, beyond the elixir of books. The only reality, for him, for now, was the family within the walls of his home, and the familiar territory of his editing work.

"I'll stay in touch," he said, in the silence that followed. "Call me, text me, anytime. I'm not moving away. We're still the best of friends. I just need a break—from everyone. Try to understand."

"We'll try, Charlie," said Louise.

"Don't be a stranger," said Theresa.

Sybil said nothing.

"Okay, book buddies," he said, with a cheerfulness he could barely muster. "Over and out."

Quickly, before anyone responded, Charlie moved his cursor over the toolbar at the bottom of his computer screen, tapped the "Mute" and "Stop Video" buttons, and left the meeting.

March 5, 2021

What is a person's life but a series of incidents?

I was thinking this as I woke up this morning—perhaps as a result of a dream I had about stringing my life together as though it were multiple strands that I could physically touch, manipulate, and meld together in a sort of pattern, like a necklace—or a quilt.

Taken all together, these strands of incidents make up my life—but do they form a recognizable pattern, or is that just wishful thinking on my part? Perhaps these multiple incidents—year upon year of daily and hourly activities—are just a mishmash of personal history, with no pattern and no reasonable connection. If that is so, what is the value of one's individual life? Who benefits from that individual life, aside from those born to that individual, those whose existence helps to sustain the human population? And, if that is so, shouldn't one's goal be to reproduce oneself as many times as possible? What else, one could argue, is the point of existence? Of course, leaving behind as many progeny as possible is not, in our advanced civilization, the only point of existence. We are here to build upon the moral, cultural, and material advances that we have inherited. We are here to learn, to understand, to practice and, finally, to teach what we have gathered together from the incidents of our lives. In the end, we are all destined to teach, whether conventionally or by example.

Is that the essence of existence, then? To make sense of what, for me and for each individual, is a series of incidents that add up to a pattern of existence that we can leave behind? Perhaps it's not my individual life that forms the pattern, but all of our lives together. Perhaps we are each a strand of existence that, if formed carefully and mindfully, will keep the necklace from breaking, the quilt from falling apart.

March 13, 2021

One year ago, my stay-at-home lockdown date happened to be Friday the 13th. I went out in the afternoon, stocked up on groceries at TJ's, filled the tank with gas, ran a couple of errands. Then I went home, and there I've stayed ever since—with some limited in-car excursions.

I've now had a first vaccine, and it looks as though my get-out-of-jail card will be good by about the middle of next month. That's hopeful.

Was it worth it? It was, although it has been a long and lonely year. What has helped to get me through it? Writing, of course. That's my oxygen. I have a manuscript that might grow up to be a book. I have supportive family and friends. A routine that gives me focus and a plan for most days. A regular dose of yoga. FaceTime and Zoom. A cozy nest of a home and, within that home, a canine companion who is a good listener and doesn't seem to mind my off-and-on approach to housekeeping. As to that, I keep the kitchen and bathroom clean, the bed made, belongings in mostly orderly condition, and let the dust fall where it may—until I'm motivated to launch a vacuum/Swiffer attack.

In terms of following politics, I was addicted for most of the year and am only now moving away from hourly and sometimes minute-by-minute reading, listening, watching. The news was often, for me, terrifying and horrifying, and I use those words deliberately. There was a steady flood of "breaking news"—from lockdown through January 6 and beyond—much of it generated by an out-of-control pandemic and an out-of-control president.

As we recover from multiple political tsunamis and, with a new administration, begin to experience a day-by-day calming of the waters, I have returned to a more normal news infusion. I know what's going on but I'm not in perpetual crisis mode. It's quite a relief.

We have all been subjected to the same political turmoil, and the same life-sucking pandemic. It's not over, but it's better. We're not coming together politically, but we're coming back to relative health and freedom of movement.

May God watch over the families and friends of those who lost their lives during this pandemic, and keep us safe as we carefully and with deliberation return to our blessedly "ordinary" lives.

March 24, 2021

As sometimes happened in their long history of friendship and discussion, the book club had decided—following Charlie's abrupt departure in February—to read a second book by the same author during the coming month.

"We're moving from the fascism of *The Plot Against America* to the radicalism of *American Pastoral,*" said Sybil, after they had assembled on Zoom. "As Charlie would have said, how in *hell* did Roth manage to be so prescient?"

"The irony of the title is devastating," said Louise. "It's an authentic American tragedy."

"I don't know," said Theresa. "Roth gets so damned side-tracked. I'm ready to turn to nonfiction for a change."

"Next month," said Louise.

"It's like coming down off a high, finishing that book," said Sybil.

"Yes, it was quite a read," said Louise.

Sitting ramrod-straight at her dining room table, wearing the imposing mantle of the lifelong teacher used to having her own way, Theresa glowered at them.

"It's just a book," she said. "A damn good book, but still—"

"It's why we're here," said Louise. "To read books and discuss what we read."

"If I've got it right," said Theresa, "we're going back in time to the '60s to get some understanding of what went on at the Capitol earlier this year. We read *The Plot Against America* to shed some light on the election, and now we're having a go at domestic terrorism. That's asking a lot of an author."

"Who better than Philip Roth?" said Louise. "He's a master novelist who goes deep into the American psyche."

"I wish Charlie were here," said Sybil. "I'd love to get his perspective."

"Well, he's not," said Theresa. "He chose not to be here, and we're perfectly capable of discussing this book without him."

Sybil was silent, not angry, but somehow crushed by Theresa's dismissal of Charlie, by her hard reasonableness. She raked a hand through her short dark hair as she formulated a response.

She missed more than Charlie's arbitration skills. She missed Charlie himself, friend and would-be lover. She missed the Charlie who had put his hand over hers in the coffee shop that afternoon in early 2020, before the world was turned upside down by the pandemic, by a president gone berserk, by the Capitol riot that, incredibly, most everyone involved seemed to have gotten away with. She had read *American Pastoral* with intense concentration, a vertical indentation between her brows, the story unfolding page by page, layer upon layer, until she got to the core, or what she thought was the core, and found—nothing. Except there, on the next page, was another multi-layered story, equally enticing, equally missing its core. Until she came to the end of the book, exhausted, having followed its mysteries for 423 pages, having solved—nothing.

Louise stepped in, missing Charlie herself but not wanting to arbitrate a spat between Theresa and Sybil.

"I have a broken history of reading Roth's novels, but I was impressed, sometimes stunned, by his writing, the thought behind the writing, the emotion behind the thought ..."

"Yes," Sybil agreed, "he does get sidetracked, as Theresa says, but it's so amazing where he goes! There's a freedom in his writing that's breathtaking."

Apropos of nothing, Theresa remarked, "I do like his use of the semicolon. It makes his endless sentences tolerable."

The other two women laughed.

"But do we ever understand what has happened in the book—or what happened at the Capitol?" asked Sybil. "Do we ever come to understand domestic terrorism—how it seeds itself and grows and destroys?"

"I don't know, Sybil," Louise answered slowly. "I don't think Roth knows. I don't think he wants us to *think* we know. He mentions somewhere toward the end that people seem to 'run out of their own being.' That's as close as he comes to an explanation, I think."

"Nonsense," said Theresa. "There are lots of clues, lots of ways he leads us to form our own conclusions."

"And what are yours, Theresa?" asked Louise.

"That bad things happen to good people, and there's nothing we can do about it."

"But the *radicalism*," said Sybil, impatient, insistent. "Where does that come from? Merry Levov doesn't become a radical just because she stutters, and her father was a sports hero and her mother was Miss New Jersey. She has everything, including the unquestioning love of her parents, and she winds up killing four people, and destroying her family."

"Roth wants us to question everything," said Louise. "He doesn't have the answers, doesn't pretend to have the answers, but the questions are eye-popping, mind-blowing. He questions goodness, virtue, ambition, goals—the frailty and abuse of the best *intentions*."

"All of it to probe the mystery of 'the monster daughter,'" said Sybil.

"Yes," said Louise, nodding her head vigorously. "Everything from first word to last is meant to try to make sense of 'the monster daughter'—the treasured child who became a radical—and, in the end, *to fail* to make sense of it."

"He says somewhere," Sybil added, "that being wrong is being human—that's how we know we're alive. We're wrong."

"So, everybody in the novel is *wrong*?" Theresa asked, her voice rising ominously.

"Yes," Sybil replied. "*Everybody* gets it wrong. In the end, there is no right. There's only wrong."

Louise realized, at that moment, how important Charlie was to their group. With only herself between Sybil and

Theresa, there were bound to be angry words, disagreements, stalemates. With his cheerful presence, his wisecracks, his protectiveness toward Sybil, Charlie had done more to keep their meetings on target than Louise had realized. He was missed, and not just by Sybil. Louise missed his critiques, which came from a mix of film industry experience and a certain reverence for books—including the many books he had not and would never read. With more of an "outsider's" view than the three of them, as someone who saw the world through a film lens most of the time, he brought his own brand of insight to the dusty world of books.

"It's hard to write about goodness," Sybil remarked. "It's easier to write about evil, about people who are evil, and nobody in this book is evil—not even 'the monster daughter.'"

"That's right," said Louise. "The wrongness shoots up in their midst like an invasive species. They can't stop it; they can't control it; they can't make it go away."

"I wish this book would go away," said Theresa. "It's so convoluted it made me feel seasick."

"It *is* a lot like being seasick," said Louise, refusing to take on Theresa's challenge, "that feeling of never getting to the end of a sentence, let alone a chapter, of never seeing the shoreline ahead, of being stuck in a boat that's tossing and turning and going nowhere. I felt like that a lot!"

Theresa was silent, having no one to disagree with. She was frustrated. The book was convoluted, and Theresa's mind was as clean and sharp as a kitchen knife. She wanted to cut through the crap. She wanted answers, and there were none. She was motivated to finish the novel because she was sure that *eventually* Roth would unravel the mystery of radicalism, would achieve the ordering of the disorderly that is one of the hallmarks of the novel form. But that was not to be. On a number of occasions, as she read the novel, Theresa's impulse was to hurl the book at a wall, but she summoned just enough curiosity, just enough patience, to see it through to the end—at which time she *did* throw the book at the fireplace wall, a target she was sure could absorb the weight of Roth's inconclusive dissertation on radicalism and its effect on a family in quiet upstate New Jersey.

Sybil was speaking.

"One of his favorite words in this book is 'secret.' Everyone is secretive. Everyone has a secret. Everyone is hiding behind a secret. Maybe he's saying that if we could only reveal our secrets, we'd have the answers he's so careful *not* to give us."

"Maybe," said Theresa, "or maybe it's just avoiding the fact that he can't bring this story to any logical conclusion, so he just stops."

"Even the way he '*stops*' the story is masterful," Sybil shot back. "As with everything else that happens in the novel, we're left more or less in the dark, because there is no 'logical' conclusion."

"Damn it all, why can't he tie up the loose ends?" Theresa responded gruffly. "There's no *satisfaction* in the read."

"There's the satisfaction of good writing," said Louise. "No answers, but emotional entanglement of the first order."

"I agree," said Sybil.

Theresa spoke up, eager to conclude the discussion.

"'Nuff said. Let's move on. We haven't read nonfiction for more than a year. It's time for a change. Even Charlie would agree with me there."

Sybil, perhaps because of a lingering protest against Theresa, perhaps because Charlie had been invoked, was quick to protest.

"But can Charlie, or Philip Roth, or anyone else, tell us *why* the Capitol riot happened? Does any of this tell us who those people are who came to the Capitol to destroy it, with the intention of killing some of those inside, rather than let the legitimate election verification proceed?"

Louise, smiling, raised her right hand, as though she were in class and was volunteering an answer.

"Perhaps it doesn't tell us who they are, but I think the book tells us something about why they came to the Capitol and why they did what they did."

Neither woman spoke up, so Louise continued.

"Philip Roth's representation of terrorism can be traced to people who were willing to go to extreme lengths to protest the Vietnam War—a war that went on for twenty long years. The Capitol riot—after you factor in Trump's deliberate provocation—can be traced to the clout of social media. Why? Because, like the monster daughter's radical friends, like Trump himself, social media bombards us with its own version of reality—the reality we *choose*!

"Whatever we believe in, whatever we track online, social media feeds back to us again and again—and the more it feeds us, the more we feel validated—which is why our choices are reflected in the information we're offered— from Facebook to Twitter feed to Google searches and on and on ...

"Eventually, for some, this can lead to extremism and, ultimately, given the right circumstances, it can lead to terrorism—the kind of terrorism that destroyed a young girl and her family in *American Pastoral*—that almost destroyed the Capitol.

"What Roth is telling us, no matter how indirectly, is that we're all vulnerable and we've all, somehow, got it wrong. If he were still around, he'd have a story to tell about last year's election—about this year's insurrection. No easy answers—sorry, Theresa—but a deep dive into yet another impending American tragedy."

March 31, 2021

I don't know where I am in this strange chronicle. I seem to be winding down. I've had my second vaccine and, as of today, I'm supposedly protected—as protected as one can be in a world still riding this pandemic—gaining ground but not there yet, nowhere near the finish line.

I feel held back, somehow, inside a cage with the door open but an unknowable threat out there, where I want to be. It's a residual fear, I know, but it's real. I feel it.

I still can't go near my family. I'm protected but they are not; vaccinated people can still carry infection to others. When will this come to even a semi-final conclusion?

I'm not a depressive sort of person, but I'm in a slump, physically, emotionally, creatively. This isolation has been so protracted—one year plus two weeks. On and on. Like a prisoner keeping track of the days with markings on the wall: one vertical mark, two, three, four—cross-slash top left to bottom right for the fifth day—start again.

It's spring. California is beautiful, glorious. I have jasmine blooming in my back yard, lavender and multi-colored daisies blossoming in my front yard. I have food, shelter, the necessities. I have family nearby. I have Indi. I have access to the outside world, a car, and magically responsive electronic devices. I have nothing, really, to complain about. So why am I keying in, word by word, my angst?

I'm grateful. There. I can say it. I'm grateful for the gift of life, which I've managed to sustain over the past dangerous months. I'm grateful for the health of my family, my friends, my associates, the strangers I talk to on the phone when I call my telephone company or my insurance rep. I'm truly grateful.

But I can't yet make my way through the open door of my cage. Something dense, slog-like, holds me back, weighs me down. I want to curl up in the back of that cage, as far from the door as I can get, and continue to watch, and wait ...

April 2, 2021

It's the second hour of the Good Friday meditation that lasts from 12:00 to 3:00 p.m.—the three hours that Jesus hung on the cross. Within that time, another Capitol guard has been killed, a second severely injured, and the attacker—a young man who crashed his car into the Capitol barrier and went at the guards with a knife—is dead from gunshot. The Capitol complex was in lockdown during the course of the incident, and the assailant was stopped—at the cost of another innocent life.

The Capitol is no longer a safe haven—and the blame lies squarely with the man who was elevated to the status of President of the United States for four years, lost the election last November, and has divided, embittered, and enraged the nation since then. He has yet to concede the election and probably never will admit his defeat or accept any responsibility for the irreparable damage he has inflicted on the country, as well as the Constitution he swore on the Bible, before all the world, to preserve, protect, and defend.

April 20, 2021

3:45 p.m. Derek Chauvin has been found guilty on all counts for the murder of George Floyd. What a triumph!

We were geared up for a less-than-guilty verdict, and for all the mayhem that might have followed. Instead, we can all enjoy a moment of relief, of satisfaction, of thankfulness for that jury of twelve men and women who made the only decision that made any sense.

This past year has been about the pandemic, but also about Black Lives Matter. When George Floyd's daughter said, "My daddy changed the world," she was speaking prophetically.

While this won't magically bring our country together, it will bring some alleviation to the suffering of the non-white races in this country who have been burdened with injustice for centuries. Now we need to pass the Voting Rights Bill, with John Lewis's name in front of it, to assure that every adult in this country can vote. And we can begin to get rid of the Republican voter amendments that, since last November, have infested almost every state in our supposed "union."

We are no longer a nation administered by white Anglo-Saxons, despite the efforts of the far right to bring back those days. We are no longer a predominantly white nation. In a few years, the non-white citizens among us will be in the majority. We can't suppress that fact with fear-mongering and worse.

Listening to the judge reading out the verdicts while watching the masked face of Derek Chauvin, I wondered, again, what was behind those eyes that had so casually observed the small crowd around him as, knee on neck, he squeezed the life out of the helpless, handcuffed George Floyd, whose last words were, "*I can't breathe.*"

May 3, 2021

Statistics: LA

Los Angeles County reported zero new coronavirus-related deaths on Sunday, and only a few hundred new cases. This would be the first time no new deaths have been reported in LA County in more than 410 days—or so I've read—with California posting the lowest virus rates in the country. It looks as though we may be over the worst of it.

⌒

Statistics: India

Meanwhile, in India, medical trainees are being pulled from their studies to help bring under control the world's biggest coronavirus surge. Both doctors and nurses in training have put their education on hold while they struggle to sustain a health system that is unable to cope with the current caseload. Hospitals, morgues, and crematoriums are reporting more than 300,000 cases per day for the past 10 days.

⌒

One side of the world takes a deep breath of relief while the other side of the world scrambles to survive. I want to feel hopeful but how can I, with India, Africa, Indonesia, and other countries breathless and suffering?

May 7, 2021

United States Covid-19 Statistics
Cases: 32,606,066
Deaths: 580,068

I haven't looked at national statistics for a while, but those numbers keep climbing. Every source tracking the numbers has different statistics, but the bottom line is close, and concerning. Are we really going to reach 600,000 dead in the U.S. before the death count levels out? Will it ever come to a standstill, or will it just go undercover, surfacing from year to year, like the flu?

The National Archives, recalling the flu pandemic of 1918, says that, with no vaccine available, people were advised to "*isolate, quarantine, practice good personal hygiene, and limit social interaction.*" Hauntingly familiar language in that recommendation. The difference? We have a vaccine—but must persuade many Americans to take it. The difference? We have made the pandemic a political issue in the United States. The difference? We seem not to have absorbed the lessons of 1918–1920.

Why are we unable to absorb the lessons of the past? There's so much we could learn if we would just listen to the voice of history. But that hasn't happened, might never happen. The Internet, our lifeline for information, is spreading disinformation simultaneously, and the disinformation is infecting not just our country but countries around the globe. The pandemic has become inextricably linked with the political. Our democracy is as much at risk as is our health. We are facing a hellish fight to maintain our freedoms—especially our voting rights. It all merges together and it's all one—an infectious disease that permeates our bodies, our minds, our souls. I can no longer clearly define the point at which one ends and the other begins.

May 13, 2021

Today, Thursday, noonish, exactly fourteen months after I began my personal lockdown, is the moment for the logical conclusion of this chronicle. The CDC has just lifted all mask restrictions for fully vaccinated Americans; in effect, the pandemic is over for those of us who have followed guidelines and have been awaiting a time when our lives can resume in a more or less normal way.

I am not ready to throw open my front door and march outside, exchanging fist bumps with my neighbors and fellow dog walkers. I do, however, feel a sense of relief, a sense of completion, a sense of coming full circle. At least symbolically, we, as a country, are approaching the end of a long journey. For me, it's still a symbolic end because it has not been tested and anything might happen in the days and weeks to come. I think of India, and I wonder how we can celebrate when they are suffering so much.

I am grateful, however, that we have reached this juncture. I can draw a deep breath of relief and feel a great sense of thankfulness. The dark and infectious radicalism that Trump released into the American psyche continues to poison the air we breathe, but the coronavirus is exiting from among us—still deadly in many parts of the world but retreating from within the boundaries of our country.

At 1:00 p.m. (4:00 p.m. ET), I watched the president and VP, maskless, confirm the message in the Rose Garden—scene of one of the most shameful maskless gatherings in the midst of the pandemic. The air in the Rose Garden has been cleansed. Hopefully, as we resume our normal lives, the air we breathe will be similarly cleansed.

July 4, 2021

"I don't care what you think. I don't want her here."

Joan faced Charlie, arms crossed, slim legs in shorts, sandaled feet firmly grounded, looking, to Charlie, formidable but emphatically attractive as they stood in a shaded corner of their back yard, away from the guests who were arriving by twos and threes for Charlie and Joan's annual 4th of July gathering.

"What am I supposed to do—she's already here," Charlie replied, calmly enough.

Joan turned her head away from him, the movement sharp, disapproving.

"You shouldn't have invited her in the first place."

"She and Louise and Theresa are my good friends, have been for a dozen years. I couldn't not invite her and Greg, and there was *no reason* not to invite them. You're making something out of nothing at all."

"Do you think I've forgotten you spent an entire afternoon with her? You started out at a café. How do I know where you ended up?"

"We've been over this, again and again. It was a friendly meeting, when she needed a friend. That's it."

Sybil and Greg waved and started walking toward them. Joan and Charlie joined them, using hand gestures, nods, and fist bumps to replace the handshakes and hugs that were no longer common.

"So good to see you, Joan," said Sybil. "You too, Charlie."

"Thanks for coming," said Joan, politely. "How are you, Greg?"

"Off duty for a change, thank God," said Greg. He looked large and healthy, handsomely tanned for a hard-working physician, at ease in casual trousers and short-sleeved shirt.

"Let me get you a beer," said Charlie, leading Greg off to the patio tables laden with food and drinks. "See you later, Sybil."

Joan and Sybil stood silent for a few moments, watching their husbands walk away from them.

"Louise and Theresa are over there," said Joan, speaking up when Sybil did not. She pointed to a shaded area beneath the largest tree in the yard, where the two women sat on a bench apart from the other guests, most of whom were gathered around the barbecue grill and food tables. The two women were eating from plates on their laps and talking comfortably with each other.

"Thanks. I'll join them," said Sybil, relieved to move away from her hostess, who seemed more than usually tense. She and Joan had very little to say to each other, but she'd never been so clearly rebuffed. It was one of the first outings for her and Greg since the beginning of the pandemic. She wanted to enjoy herself, to mingle with friends and strangers, to be in Charlie's company in a casual, unstrained way. Greg was the most unsuspicious of men; she was not worried about him. It was Joan who worried her.

"It's all very surreal, this gathering together as of old," she said, sitting down with Louise and Theresa, her plate of barbecued rib, bean salad, and crudités balanced on her lap.

"Heavenly, and a little scary," said Louise. "Do you suppose everyone here is vaccinated?"

"We are," said Theresa, "and we're outside. I think we're okay."

"Last time we were here was for their 4th of July party in 2019," said Sybil. "Can you believe it?"

"Eons ago," said Louise.

"Pretty much the same time, same place, same people, and yet …"

Sybil stopped mid-sentence.

"I know what you mean," said Louise. "The same and yet—so very different."

Sybil cleared her throat and asked, without looking at her friends, "Do you think Charlie will come back to our book club meetings?"

"Hard to say," said Theresa. "Joan keeps the hook in but gives him a pretty long lead—although lately there seems to have been 'a twitch upon the thread.'"

"But why?" asked Sybil, her voice high and plaintive. "What have we done?"

Louise and Theresa chose not to respond. They nibbled at their food and looked around the yard, distracted by the novelty of being with people who were gathered to enjoy themselves, to eat and drink and chat standing or seated close together, mostly without masks—there were a few holdouts— on a warm, breezy California evening, in what they hoped was a post-pandemic world, at least in the United States of America.

Charlie's two boys, with four or five young friends, raced past them, Fido barking joyfully behind them. The sun was still above the horizon, its rays splashing onto the guests as they raised their voices to be heard over the music on the loudspeaker Charlie had rigged up for the occasion. His usual whacky diversity ranged from Billie Eilish to Kool & the Gang. The latter were live at the Hollywood Bowl that evening, no doubt reprising their own "Celebration."

The back yard of the West Hollywood house was not large but neatly enclosed with privacy fencing and graced with several trees—one of which, an old acacia, was shading the three book club friends. They watched the children circle the yard, then disappear into the house, doubtless to the boys' bedroom with its large yellow 'Keep out' sign nailed to the door.

"Shouldn't we mingle?" asked Louise, after they'd finished eating.

"I like it here," said Theresa, "and I barely know anyone over there, except for Greg."

"We know Charlie," said Sybil.

"Yes, but he's busy being a host," said Theresa.

"Greg seems to be enjoying himself," commented Louise, after observing the animated group of guests on the patio.

"He's a good mixer," said Sybil. "He can fit in anywhere."

"We're just a corner of Charlie's life," Louise added, philosophically. "Once a month or so, for a few hours, talking about books—not that important in the scheme of things."

"What's not important?" asked Sybil. "The books—or us?"

"Both, I suppose," said Louise. "We've been coming here for years, for the 4th and a few of our book club meetings, but when has Joan made us feel really welcome?"

Theresa seemed to accept this response, but Sybil squirmed on the bench, as if in protest.

"I don't think Charlie will drop us," Sybil exclaimed.

"Not unless Joan puts her foot down," said Theresa.

"I would guess she's already done that," said Louise. "I say we're only here because Charlie insisted on it."

"Do you really think so?"

Sybil turned to Louise, her eyes wide, her voice almost pleading. Louise looked at her much younger friend with pity and affection. She was about to say something that she had thought about for some time, something she felt Sybil needed to hear. It was, perhaps, not the best time to say it but, then again, when was the best time to say something potentially hurtful?

"We're being tolerated as guests," said Louise. "Greg isn't part of our club so he's center stage. But Joan won't be rushing over here any time soon to urge us to fill up our plates again and say hello to their friends."

"If that's the case, why don't we leave?" asked Theresa, whose response was always practical.

"Not till after the fireworks," said Sybil, leaning back and crossing her arms. "I'm not going to sneak out with my tail between my legs."

Louise nodded.

"As long as you understand what's going on here."

Just then, Charlie broke away from the group he was talking to and headed across the lawn toward them, gripping four chilled beer bottles.

"Haven't had a chance to sit with you," he said, handing off the beer and pulling a lawn chair close to them. He sat down with a sigh and raised his bottle. "Cheers. Glad you could come."

"We're glad to be here," said Sybil eagerly—too eagerly. "It's so wonderful to be out and about again, don't you think?"

"I don't think I could have stayed cooped up much longer," Charlie replied, glancing over his shoulder at the guests clustered on the patio. Joan turned toward them and waved, then turned back to their guests. Charlie raised the beer to his lips and took a long drink, his throat working visibly.

"Joan needed this," he said. "I think the boys, myself, this long goddamned hiatus from everything else, has gotten to her."

"She's a wonderful hostess, as always," said Louise. "Everything's perfect."

Charlie looked at her, then at Theresa. His eyes glanced over Sybil; then he stood up.

"I'd better get back to the grill," he said.

"Tell Greg I'll be right there," said Sybil.

"Will do."

⌒

When it was full dark, when the hungry guests were sated and the sounds of early fireworks were filling the air, the children cracked and shook their red, white, and blue glow sticks and, with yelps and cries of excitement, ran out onto the lawn.

"Poor Generation Alpha spawn," said Charlie, his voice clear and serene in the darkness. "They'll never know the rush a kid can get lighting a sparkler or watching firecrackers and smoke bombs go off in their own back yard."

"Better safe than minus a finger or an eye," said Greg.

The guests sat on or near the patio, every suitable chair in the house and yard having been enlisted for the party. Greg sat on Charlie's swivel office chair, pushing the seat lazily from side to side as he chatted with Charlie, Joan, and one or two other guests who sat nearby. Louise, Theresa, and Sybil had moved among the guests before they again formed their own grouping, this time with Sybil and Theresa on the patio swing, Louise on a folding chair across from them.

"What we'll see—mostly hear," said Joan, "will be from a distance but safe for all concerned—downtown, the Hollywood Bowl—maybe some of our less cautious neighbors."

"Isn't that what we're all about now?" said Charlie. "Being safe—as in inoculated, insulated—isolated?"

Mike, one of Charlie's work associates, a giant of a man with a gentle voice, spoke into the darkness.

"I, for one, am okay with isolation and its consequences. Every member of my immediate family is healthy, functioning. We lost two close friends and they'll be missed, but we survived; our family survived. That's something."

The guests murmured their assent. Some of them had recently started going out socially for the first time since the start of the pandemic. Others had taken a more casual approach or, like Greg, were propelled by their professions to mix. No one among the group of friends gathered on the patio, their faces softly lit with the scented candles placed around them, was a defiant anti-masker or anti-vaccine advocate. They were united in their support of the pandemic precautions and prohibitions. Charlie, like many others in his social and economic class, had found that the pandemic, and the political drama surrounding it, had solidified a kind of polarization—appalling in its implications for the future—based not only on insurmountable individual differences but on hard-core geographical divides.

Which was why, when a female voice was clearly heard to say, "Fuck it," a surge of energy seemed to electrify the guests.

A few of the children nearby stopped in their tracks, always happy to hear "grownups" curse—especially when it involved blunt four-letter exclamations of anger, disgust, or impatience.

Charlie put his arm around the woman sitting next to him.

"What's your gripe, Alice, my lovely?" he asked. "Is it the pandemic, or has Joan run out of ice cream cones?"

Joan stood in the doorway to the kitchen holding an insulated Styrofoam container lined with ice chips. Inside the container were old-fashioned sugar cones topped with one smoothly rounded scoop of vanilla ice cream. The ice cream cones were a traditional treat served during the fireworks display at Charlie and Joan's gatherings. The children, who had been looking out for it, came running to snatch up the cones.

Alice, middle-aged, solidly built, buxom in bright red tee-shirt, pugnacious after more than her share of beer, grinned at Joan and gave Charlie a friendly punch on the shoulder.

"I'm so almighty sick of this fucking pandemic and all of its prohibitions and restraints," she said, taking the cone Joan handed to her. "What good has any of it done? We lost 600,000 of our people, for Christ's sake! How much worse could it get? We didn't do any better than we did in 1918, when we had no vaccine and no restrictions to speak of. And now we're begging and bribing people to take the vaccine! The whole thing makes me crazy."

The children had run out on the lawn again with glow sticks in one hand, cones in the other. Joan had gone back to the kitchen for another round of cones. The guests stirred in their seats, alert again after an excess of food and beer, ready for whatever was in contention.

"You're a teacher, Alice," said Charlie. "Do you think you and Joan and your fellow educators should have gone on with school during the past year?"

"Who knows?" said Alice. "Good or bad, wrong or right, the damage has been done—and for what? There's no making up this past academic year—distance learning on steroids is what I called it. If we'd kept the schools open, with masks and social distancing, the odds are we'd be in about the same place we are now—and the kids wouldn't have lost a year of class time, a lot of free meals for the those who depended on them, and all the benefits of being in the society of their peers."

Before anyone had a chance to respond, Alice went on, her voice rising above the sound of fireworks in the distance.

"But that's not all that got fucked up this past year," she said. "This social distancing thing has become more than a safety measure; it's now a way of life. We don't *want* to be physically close to each other anymore; we're comfortable with our isolation. It works for us so—what the hell—let's just live this way from now on. Let's just live in our goddamn bubbles forever and ever."

"Alice, I think you've nailed it," said Charlie, getting up and making his way to the kitchen door. "I'm going to check on the ice cream delivery service."

⌒

"You should be outside with our guests," said Joan.

"Somehow, I think it's more important to be here in the kitchen, with you," said Charlie.

"I can't imagine why. I guess I can slap a few ice cream cones together without your help."

"I'm sure you can. It's the explosives I'm worried about."

"What are you talking about?"

"You, Joan. I'm talking about you. If I lit a match right now, close to you, you'd go off like a firecracker."

"Don't exaggerate."

Joan stopped, ice cream scoop in mid-air, and focused her attention on her husband. She didn't say anything. Charlie knew he would have to speak first.

"Look, Joan, tonight's kind of a finale for me and the book club ladies. I know it. They know it. I already told them I was backing out. We've had a good run and now I'm moving on. So don't spoil it for me or for them. I'll always choose you. You know that, don't you?"

She pushed the scoop into the hard-packed ice cream, drew out a glistening white ball, and pushed it firmly down onto the sugar cone she held in her left hand. Charlie took the cone and positioned it in the iced Styrofoam container. They repeated the process again, and then again, and Charlie realized that this careful and precise repetition was the very foundation of their marriage, and that he wanted, above all, for it—the repetition and the marriage—to go on.

This day, this evening of congeniality and distant fireworks, marked the beginning of their post-pandemic life together. In August, the boys would go back to school and Joan would go back to teaching. He was already doing some of his film editing at the studio. Their lives were once again on track, or about to be on track. For their sakes, for the sake of his marriage—his second and, hopefully, his last marriage—he would turn his back on the book club. Louise and Theresa seemed to have accepted this, but Sybil couldn't let go. He was aware that Joan sensed this—and that it made her furious.

Outside, on the patio, the three friends listened to Alice, with her grim assessment of the post-pandemic mindset, and Mike, with his moderate responses. They listened as the other guests chose to agree or argue with them. Theresa agreed with most of what Alice had to say but she chose not to speak. Her mind was on Turk, and the last 4th of July they had been here together, holding hands in the dark as the fireworks exploded all around them. She wondered if it was worthwhile to carry on in a post-pandemic world without Turk. Louise was amused by Alice's pugilistic approach to their current culture wars, but not willing—or perhaps not ready—to defend the fragile moral and political victory personified by Joe Biden. She simply hoped for it to continue. The alternative was, for her, unthinkable. Sybil was silent, pensive.

Charlie came outside with more cones, handing them out with his usual good humor to "the book club ladies"—addressing them as "Empress" Theresa, "Prime Minister" Louise, and "Princess" Sybil. Sybil could barely summon a response. She seemed to be caught up in the tension between Charlie and Joan—an unintended victim unable to circumvent the snare, like a dolphin trapped in a fishing net.

At last the fireworks display died down and the guests began their departures, gathering up their children and their emptied casserole dishes. Greg, gregarious to the end, came for Sybil and escorted her out of the yard. Theresa left almost hurriedly, after breaking her own rule and giving Charlie a brief hug. Charlie and Joan stood next to each other while their guests said their *thankyous* and *goodbyes*. Finally, only Louise remained, gathering up plates, beer bottles, and Dixie cups.

"You don't have to do that," said Joan, as she went into the house. "But thank you. Thanks for coming. I'm going to put the boys to bed."

"Sit with me," said Charlie, motioning Louise to the patio swing. They sat down, side by side, surrounded by darkness, flickering candles, a wash of light from the kitchen window, listening to a nearby whistling firecracker, the periodic boom from late-night displays invisible to them—then listening to the silence that was like a prelude to the next spectacle of sound.

"I'm glad you stayed," said Charlie. "I didn't have much of a chance to talk earlier."

Louise waited for him to go on, thinking about their many book club meetings on Zoom during the pandemic, and the many years of meetings before that, at each other's homes. Charlie hosted once or twice a year—fewer than the others, but he was always working around Joan's schedule, or the boys' activities, or his work. Louise wondered if he would miss their meetings.

"I'll miss being with you and Theresa—and Sybil," he said, as if in answer to her unspoken thought. "It's been a good run."

"It doesn't have to stop," said Louise.

"Yes. It does."

"Okay. I get it. But you're always welcome back."

"That's the thing about you, Louise. You *get it*. I don't have to explain things to you. You just—get it."

They sat in the darkness, in silence except for the diminished sounds of an almost-normal 4th of July—mindful that it was following on the heels of a pandemic, a disastrous presidency, a disputed election, a Capitol insurrection of monumental proportions.

All around them, in the darkness, were the sights and sounds of the past year—a year of such profound change that Louise and Charlie could not yet analyze it. It was too close. But they knew, in their own way, what they had lost—and found. For Charlie, it was the loss of Nate, a close friend and mentor—victim of the coronavirus—and the loss of a certain amount of personal freedom, in exchange for his wife's peace of mind. For Louise, it was the realization that she was living in a world with no moral certitude, no inoculation against corruption, no safe ground. There was only a sort of glossing over of reality—a pathetic attempt to make meaningful a year of what was, in the end, incomprehensible.

Is there a God watching over us? she thought to herself. *Without a God, there is no understanding all of this; there is only acceptance.*

Louise and Charlie sat side by side on the patio swing, gliding gently back and forth, as they pondered but did not say what was in their thoughts. Charlie put his arm around Louise's shoulders; she leaned into him, happy for his warmth, his touch. The great untouchable year was over— but so much had ended as well.

July 4, 2021

My imperfect heart has survived the pandemic, and all of the greater and lesser demands on a body that reached its peak years ago and persists in survival mode.

Like many others, I'm grateful for my survival but unsure about what lies ahead, both for me and for a country that has endured so much tragedy and so much political division since I started this journal on April 1, 2020. I'm bringing my chronicle to a close today, on the 4th of July, 2021, when many of my countrymen and women are celebrating our newfound "freedom" from mask-wearing and sheltering in place. But I'm uncertain about our survival as a democracy and our continuing as the richest and most fruitful land in this Covid-devastated world.

Covid-19 and its ugly variants are still a looming threat, here and in many other parts of the world. I grieve for India, Africa, Indonesia. Meantime, many Americans are unwilling to get the vaccine that is free, readily available, and could save their lives. President Biden's goal was to have 70 percent of the population vaccinated by the 4th of July. He got to 67.1 percent, close enough but indicative of the personal and political struggle between those who see the vaccine as a godsend and those who see it as something demonic and destructive. It's an insurmountable barrier of contention.

I've been following the spread of two viruses since April of 2020. As I wrote when I started this chronicle, the pandemic has been two-edged: one airborne and viral, the other political and endemic.

I've been a harsh critic of the former president, Donald Trump, and I see no indication that this will change in the future. Perhaps, as he says about Covid-19, "It's China's fault," but where then does the fault lie in the pandemic of deceit and disinformation that pervades our country? Can we say, "It's Trump's fault"? Did he initiate and fuel the disruption which culminated in the January 6, 2021, insurrection? Or is he an empty vessel into which nearly half of our population (including 74 million voters) dumped their frustration, their anger, their inability to accept our country's evolution as a multiracial culture?

I am a novelist, a writer of contemporary—not dystopian—fiction. I could not have imagined the course of this past year and a half. We have not yet beaten down the virus to manageable intensity, nor have we in any way harnessed the hatred and potential violence fueling the extremist elements among us.

I want to understand, just as I want understanding.

Epilogue

December, 2021

How hopeful and naïve I was to think that the ugliness of the past two years would go away, by presidential decree, on the 4ᵗʰ of July, 2021. Two-thirds of the country would be vaccinated, and therefore we would be well on the road back to health and prosperity.

Instead, we continue to fight not just a health crisis but an epidemic of hatred and retribution unlike anything I've witnessed in my lifetime.

Who is to blame? Can any one person bear this responsibility? Or did January 6 unleash some frighteningly destructive force within those of us who were prepared to hate, to give voice to that hatred and, in some instances, to move from the expression of hatred to actual violence?

⟿

On November 17, 2021, Representative Paul Gosar (R-AZ) was censured in the House and stripped of his committee power for releasing a video in which—using computer animation— Representative Alexandria Ocasio-Cortez (D-NY) was killed and President Joe Biden was attacked. There were 223 *yes* votes—all 221 of the House Democrats voted for the censure— while only two of the 213 House Republicans voted for censure.

Joe Biden—at least in his public appearances—remains relentlessly optimistic, despite the dip in his popularity. I do not feel, cannot pretend to be, optimistic. School board members imposing mask-wearing and other health restrictions have had their lives and the lives of their families threatened. Books like *Beloved* and *The Handmaid's Tale* have been banned in schools. Election workers are being terrorized. Expressions of hatred and racism have become more and more unrestrained.

⌒

Political analysts say that Trump will run again for president in 2024, and that his chances of winning, at this point, are fifty-fifty. When Joe Biden won the 2020 election, I thought the biggest battle was over. I was wrong. As long as Trump can convince a huge chunk of Americans that the 2020 election was "the big lie," we are still at war. The election was a critical win but not the decisive battle.

⌒

I can no longer say with confidence that we will continue with our democracy intact. With a third of our population questioning the legitimacy of last year's presidential election, with recently enacted restrictive state voting laws and gerry-mandering, we are on a path to autocracy—whether or not Donald Trump returns to power. This possibility is now part of our daily news conversation.

I am so weary of politics—but I can't escape it. Escape means turning my back on an impending democratic crisis. Whether I write about it or ignore it, it will keep moving and growing among us—like the pandemic.

And the pandemic continues to surge—wave upon wave—continuing through the 2021 holiday season. The latest wave, following Delta, is called Omicron, the fifteenth letter of the Greek alphabet. There have been a dozen variants so far: Alpha, Beta, Delta, Delta plus, Gamma, Epsilon, Eta, Iota, Kappa, Lambda, Mu, and Omicron. There's some concern that we might run out of Greek letters (there are 24) before we run out of variants. Might that be called a sick joke?

I have had many gloomy days during the past 22 months. I won't say I've been depressed. I believe that's too extreme a term for what I've felt and am feeling. I've been—disheartened. Everything I've felt and written about has to do with my ongoing struggle to somehow take hold of and understand what is happening in the world: the crises of global health and climate change, and a domestic reign of terror.

⌒

Everything hinges on everything else. For me, that is the lesson of 2020 and 2021. Any thinking adult can connect the origins of the pandemic with the loss of natural habitat and the ravages of climate change. Any reasonable adult—liberal, conservative, or somewhere in between—can connect the dots that have led to the state of our present precarious democracy. But I wonder—will that which is good in us—that which is promising and hopeful—prevail? As Louise asks, in an early Zoom book club meeting, *"But are we good?"*

⌒

Like most of us, I look back on my life with mixed emotions— gratitude for what I was fortunate enough to know and to have; regret for what I didn't know, didn't have, didn't do.

Over the years, I have come to accept and embrace my personal life choices. Although often impulsive, those choices were mostly straight from the heart and, imperfect though it is, my heart continues to be my best guide.

I've been one of the fortunate who has survived the pandemic. I'm now protected by two vaccines and a booster. I've had a long life, and perhaps will have a longer one, so that I can continue to cherish my family and friends, and to do what makes me happy—what makes me want to get up in the morning and start a new day.

What is it I do in the morning when I sit down with that first heavenly cup of hot black coffee?

I write.

Acknowledgments

Thank you, Barbara Lanctot, for your friendship, editing skills, patience, and encouragement.

Thanks to designers Judith San Nicolas (cover) and Lorie DeWorken (interior), and to photographers Jennifer Skelly and Auston James. I value your collective talent.

Special thanks to my pre-pub readers Virginia Woodrow, Barbara Potyk, Margaret Mark, and Judith Kirscht. Bless you!

As always, I am grateful for the love and support of my family, and for the friendship and creative energy of the late Holly Prado's ongoing writers' group.

About the Author

Toni Fuhrman is the author of four novels, including *Only Yesterday*, *A Windless Place*, *The Second Mrs. Price*, and *One Who Loves*. Her novels are intensely personal explorations of intimacy and obsession within the context of strong family ties. Toni grew up in the Midwest and now makes her home in Los Angeles, where she is working on her next book. Her personal essays on writing and reading are at tonifuhrman.com.

About the Publisher

A Windless Place publishes literary work in multiple genres: fiction, nonfiction, poetry, and hybrid.

A Windless Place
P. O. Box 291015
Los Angeles, CA, USA 90029

A WINDLESS PLACE

www.ingramcontent.com/pod-product-compliance
Lightning Source LLC
Chambersburg PA
CBHW021135090426
42740CB00008B/801